Processes: or a Depth Psychology

eight selected papers on

𝓟sychoanalysis

In memory of my friend Premal S. Desai, who showed me
the value of life through a smile.
– will see you again.

© 2008 by Phodis Evangelou

ISBN: 978-0-95568-500-2

Preface

Phodis Evangelou demonstrates keen enthusiasm toward the works of Sigmund Freud. Phodis is very much of the opinion that Freud was one of the most prominent figures within psychology of the early 1900's. Phodis has put together eight essays that display the insightful scientific methods that Freud initiated and developed through his life as he intended to apply a scientific explanation to the function of behaviour. This insightful book contributes to the outstanding efforts made within psychoanalysis in order to elaborate further and re-examine Freud's attempt to understand human experience on the most rudimentary level, that of the unconscious.

Contents

Section One: Five Essays on Psychoanalysis

i. Psychoanalytic School of Thought Page 5
   on the Unconscious:
   a brief contribution of
   psychological and biological evidence

ii. Freud's contribution on dreams and its Page 13
    theory of function

iii. Theory and Technique: Page 27
     Libido, Oedipus Complex and Neurosis.
     Jung and Freud's Account

iv. Winnicott's Theory of Development: Page 41
    Understanding Play as Constructing
    the Child's Personal World

v. Examining 'The Order' of the Group Page 54
   and its Formation

Section Two: Two Freudian Case Studies Re-examined

vi. **The Case of Dora:**   **Page 62**
    **Dora's first dream, her feelings
toward her mother re-examined
and Freud's failure to interpret
the transference**

vii. **The Wolf-Man:**   **Page 74**
    Belief in God the Father as the Wolf

Section Three: Considerations For a New Approach to Therapy

viii. **A Mind-Body Connection:**   **Page 85**
    **A developing theory of therapy
for people that suffer with
Wernicke's Aphasia (Damage to the
left side of the brain that processes language)**

Psychoanalytic School of Thought on the Unconscious: a brief contribution of psychological and biological evidence

"Everything fell into place, the cogs meshed, the thing really seemed to be a machine which in a moment would run of itself". (Freud's Letter to Fliess 32, Pp.129)

The theory of the unconscious according to Sigmund Freud's psychoanalytic perspective has been the subject of much debate for over a century. However, with the development of new scientific measures it is now possible to gain a more accurate reading of how the mind functions. Freud (1895) asserts that the unconscious exists and although it is not directly accessible to consciousness there is a relation between the two. According to Freud, consciousness distorts the content of the unconscious. He developed his theory on the very premise that the unconscious mind contains wishes, fears, feelings, memories and ideas that are prevented from expressing conscious awareness. They manifest themselves, instead, by their influence on conscious processes; dreams and neurotic symptoms have this effect (Freud 1911 Pp. 142).

Freud asserts that there are three divisions of the human mind, the id, the ego and the super-ego. The ego and super-ego function consciously and unconsciously, while the id functions only in the unconscious. According to the pleasure-principle the id is influenced by sex and aggression, which are instinctually rooted (Freud 1923 Pp. 499), and because of this it is suggested that the id is the most powerful of the three agents. Therefore, the ego aims to find ways in which (safe and socially acceptable) satisfy the id's desires, without transgressing the limits imposed by the superego. The ego is developed during childhood, the super ego has as its aim to apply moral values in satisfying one's wishes. This is demonstrated in Freud's work and he shows the ego as being oriented towards perceptions in the real world, where the id on the other hand, is oriented towards internal drives (Freud 1926 Pp. 16). In this respect, the ego is associated with reason, and the id is associated with the passions.

This exposes the existence of an underlying force that influences behaviour, therefore it is essential to identify this source to gain a greater understanding of its processes in order to assert a function.

Evidence that an unconscious exists is reflected in the process of transference, *'a process of actualisation of unconscious wishes'* (Laplanche and Pontalis 2006 Pp. 455). Freud demonstrated that transference emerges as *'the most powerful resistance'* to a treatment, (Freud 1911 Pp. 101). According to Freud the reason that transference exists in the first place, is due to infantile experiences that influence later life (Freud 1911 Pp. 104). If this is the case it is essential to assert the existence of an unconscious that does not only register and contain information but also influences behaviour that can be linked back to childhood.

Freud employed a technique called 'dream analysis' in order to understand abnormal behaviour that stems from unconscious processes; *'The interpretation of dreams is the royal road to a knowledge of the unconscious activities of the mind'* (Freud 1901 Pp. 608). He used "free association" to unearth memories that are buried within the unconscious. Dream analysis and free association were measures taken to understand the driving forces behind behaviour.

Freud's assumption that the unconscious mind can be measured working in ways that yield the true desires hidden in the unconscious state, could be due to the unconscious perceiving stimuli that play a major part in deep embedded fantasies and thoughts being processed that conflict with the 'moral' way of living.

A thought that is made conscious by a new focus of attention is termed preconscious, and for that reason not all mental activity of which the patient is unaware belongs to the unconscious. However, repressed memories are often translated, according to Freud, into *'screen-memories'* (Freud 1901 Pp. 43) that the ego is then able to remember. The ego has the task of bringing the influence of the external world to bear upon the id and its tendencies, and endeavours to substitute the reality-principle for the pleasure-principle.

In order to clarify and understand how the unconscious operates it is important to examine not just the psychological explanation of its function but also to gain an insight into how biological and neuronal processes contribute to its existence.

There is biological evidence that serves to demonstrate the functioning and rationale behind the unconscious, that marries up with Freud's theory of function of the unconscious. The amygdala (located deep within the cerebral cortex) has been identified as an area of the brain to store associations of feeling, such as fear. The amygdala coordinates autonomic and endocrine responses in the context of emotional states (Kandel, E. 2006 Pp. 45). Here, implicit memory serves a function of survival that is unconsciously processed. The reason for this is that if all human behaviour was consciously processed, the regulating and functioning of fear would take too much time and as a result will not be as effective in dangerous circumstances, therefore survival and reproductive rates would decline.

Joseph LeDoux suggests that the amygdala lay down unconscious memories in much the same way that the hippocampus lays down conscious ones. This leads on to the notion that unconscious memories are particularly likely to be formed during stressful events because the hormones and neurotransmitters released at such times make the amygdala more excitable. Similarly, when a stressful event is recalled the hippocampal system will produce conscious recollections while the amygdala-based system will produce a sort of physical reminiscence, reconstituting the body state (pumping heart, sweaty palms and so on) that arose with the original experience (Gazzaniga. M., et al., 2002 Pp. 554-554). Clearly this demonstrates an unconscious process present that serves a purpose in stressful times. This evidence credits Freud's notion on infantile experiences that can contribute to later life influences that can develop as a neurosis (Freud 1899 Pp. 222). However, other problems such as anxiety and post-traumatic stress could unconsciously be influenced on a biological level. If a memory is burnt into the amygdala with enough force it may be almost un-containable and trigger such dramatic bodily reactions that a person may re-experience the precipitating trauma, complete with full sensory replay. This condition, post-traumatic stress disorder, is quite clearly linked to a particular experience as are most frightening memories.

There is clearly a link between Freud's notion of the unconscious and unconscious biological processes as demonstrated by Kandel and LeDoux. Freud's theory of the formation of the id infuses biological substances on the neuron level with psychical processes, this is introduced in a Project for a Scientific Psychology (1886-1899), *'Let us recall, then, that from the first the nervous system had two functions: the reception of stimuli from outside and the discharge of excitations of endogenous origin'* (Freud

1899 Pp. 303). Freud suggests that there is continual interaction between the individual's endogenous and the exogenic world. This is demonstrated by the Permeable neurone which is *'turned towards this external world'* (Freud 1899 Pp. 304), discharges the Quantity (of the intercellular order of magnitude) penetrating to the neurones, however, it will be exposed to the effect of major Quantity (in general, or of the order of magnitude in the external world). According to Kandel (1999) a portion of mental function is owed to genes and protein synthesis, an expression that has an effect on the interconnection of neuronal synapses. According to his theory behaviour can be altered by gene modification, usually this would take the form of psychical anomalies induced by trauma; *'it follows that 'culture' can express itself as nature'* (Mancia, M. 2006 Pp. 86). It can be theorised that external influences place demands on the ego that have an effect and integrate with the unconscious biological processes, in this instance repressed memories are often translated, according to Freud, into *'screen-memories'* (Freud 1901 Pp. 43) that the ego is then able to remember. The ego has the task of bringing the influence of the external world to bear upon the id and its tendencies, and endeavours to substitute the reality-principle for the pleasure-principle which reigns in the id. Freud's notion on the construction of the unconscious incorporates the id on the level of instinctual motive urges and impulses. The very idea that it is instinctual suggests that there is a biological foundation.

It is almost certain that the unconscious plays a major part in one's life determining a person's behaviour. It is quite clear that we are far from mastering the true angle of the unconscious mind with a solid foundation, because there are so many avenues still left to be explored in this particular subject area. However, Freud's contribution of the unconscious is of great interest as he conceptualises a workable theory of the dynamics of the mind that is qualified through a theory that suggests the unconscious is partly constructed on a biological level that works in line with his notion on the unconscious. Also, with the contribution of neuronal evidence and modern day techniques applied, this is becoming more evident.

Bibliography

Freud, S. (1886-1899) Re-published in 2001, 'Pre-Psycho-Analytic Publications and Unpublished Drafts', The Standard Edition of the Complete Psychological Works, Volume 1, Vintage Publications.

Freud, S. (1900-1901) Re-published in 2001, 'The Interpretation of Dreams', The Standard Edition of the Complete Psychological Works, Volume 5, Re-published by Vintage Publications.

Freud, S. (1901) Re-published in 2001, 'The Psychopathology of Everyday Life', The Standard Edition of the Complete Psychological Works, Volume 6, Re-published by Vintage Publications.

Freud, S. (1911-1913) Re-published in 2001, 'Case History of Schreber, Papers on Technique and Other Works', The Standard Edition of the Complete Psychological Works, Volume 12, Re-published by Vintage publications.

Freud, S. (2005) The Essentials of Psycho-analysis, Selected and introduced by Anna Freud, Vintage publications.

Gazzaniga, M., Ivry. R., and Mangun, G. (2002) Cognitive Neuroscience, The Biology of the Mind, W. W. Norton and Company, New York/London.

Guttmann, G., and Scholz-Strasser, I. (1998) Freud and the Neurosciences, From Brain research to the Unconscious, Austrian Academy of Sciences Press.

Kandel, E. (2006) In Search of Memory, The Emergence of a New Science of Mind, New York/London, W. W. Norton and Company.

Mancia, M. (February 2006) The International Journal of Psychoanalysis, Volume 87, Part 1, Implicit memory and early unrepressed unconscious: Their role in the therapeutic process (How the neurosciences can contribute to Psychoanalysis), Institute of Psychoanalysis.

Freud's contribution on dreams and its theory of function

Historic account

Perhaps one of the most profound discoveries that Freud made was of understanding the formation of dreams and asserting a theory of function to it. *"Here the secret of dreams was revealed to Dr Sigm. Freud on 24 July 1895"* (Jones, E. 1961 Pp. 301).

The function of dreams has been in question throughout the ages with much mysticism surrounding the concept of how they are formed and what purpose they serve. For example, the ancient Greeks believed that dreams were some sort of spiritual insight. Each culture asserts a different meaning to dreams, and this in turn would have a direct influence on the common religion or belief in that region as it contributes to its culture. According to the New King James Bible, Genesis Chapter 41, Verses 1-36, Joseph attempts to interpret the dream of the Pharaoh of Egypt. Not only does Joseph express his understanding of the dream through assigning the content to symbolism but also foretells the future with it; verse 26, "The seven good cows are seven years, and the seven good heads are seven years; the dreams are one" (Nelson, T., 1992 Pp. 56-57). Two interesting points can be made. Firstly, the most common principle of decoding visions and dreams, according to the Prophets of the Old Testament, was to simplify the content and to attribute its meaning symbolically. The exegesis of the Hermeneutics is the principle that employs a science of interpretation that bares a systematic trend throughout the Old Testament (Kevin, J., Conner, and Malmin, K., 1983 Pp. 1). Secondly, Joseph concludes that the Pharaoh's two dreams were in fact one, the second dream being that of a continuation of the first. An interesting point here is that Freud also notes that *'all dreams that are dreamt in a single night belong in a single context,'* (Freud 1932 Pp. 55). This has been demonstrated to some extent by Franz Alexander (1925), that if presented together two dreams dreamt in one night are producing a wish-fulfilment in two stages. For example, if the dream (the wish) were to take action against someone in particular, the person will appear undisguised in the first dream and the action hinted at. However, in the second dream the person will be either unrecognisable or replaced by someone else with the intended action executed; *'where one* (dream) *represents a punishment and the other the sinful wish-fulfilment...... if one accepts the punishment for it, one can go on to allow oneself the forbidden thing'* (Freud 1932 Pp. 56).

Freud does acknowledge some of the ancient theoretical assumptions of the purpose and function of dreams. Aristotle, for example, noted that during sleep dreams give a magnified construction to small stimuli. As bodily changes such as body temperature could correlate with a dream of going through fire (Freud 1900 Pp. 3). Aristotle also noted *'that dreaming is the continuation of our mental activity into the state of sleep'* Freud then suggests that psychoanalysis combines this process with the *'recognition of the unconscious'* (Freud 1931 Pp. 209).

Freud departs from the traditional view of how dreams are interpreted and leads on to a theory of a wish to the unconscious. Although Freud's technique is universal the content of meaning would vary according to the individual. This seems like a more plausible theory of dream interpretation and through analysis this can be demonstrated.

Dream-work

In order to gain an understanding of what dreams are and how they function according to the Psychoanalytic perspective, it is important to give an account of the dream-work that Freud developed in the early 1900's. The dream-work is structured to include displacement, the replacing of latent elements by something more remote, by disguising the latent thoughts of the dream. These disguised processes are typical of primary processes. To distinguish the formation of dreams from conscious thought Freud asserts that the processes are primary in nature that precede conscious (secondary) processes. A primary process is distinguished from a secondary process on the basis that it is a *'characteristic of the unconscious system'* (Laplanche, J., and Pontalis, J.-B., 2006 Pp. 339). Within this domain of the mind psychical energy is not prohibited to flow freely as there is no constraint from the ego. Condensation and Displacement process ideas in turn to formulate and re-cathect the ideas which stem from satisfying experiences, which come from the very depths of the unconscious. This happens because latent thoughts are subject to dream censorship. Censorship is to accept or reject ideas, impulses, etc, as one of the joint functions of the ego and superego. Upon waking, remembering the content of a dream and assigning an image to represent a number of ideas, is termed as Condensation. It is assumed that the 'condensed' image is an expression of the separate images that carry symbolic meaning.

It would seem only right to record the dream as soon as possible after waking if so much importance is placed on dreams for an insight to the unconscious, however, Freud makes it clear that for the process of analysis to be effective it is important that the Analyzan makes no attempt to record the dream. *'For the resistance from which he has extorted the preservaton of the text of the dream will then be displaced onto its associations and will make the manifest dream inaccessible to interpretation'*, (Freud 1900 Pp. 42). Naturally, once the Analyzan is awake from the dream the dream content is dismantled by the Ego, *'The forgetting of dreams is a product of resistance',* (Freud 1900 Pp. 520). Resistance demonstrates a sign of conflict, and therefore it is essential that the analyst can be a witness to the Analyzan's struggle to recall.

Freud's dream of Irma's injection dated 23-24th of July 1895 (Freud 1900 Pp. 108-121) can demonstrate how Freud's methodological account of dream interpretation is put into practice. In reflection Freud notes that his dream was probably the *'anticipation'* of his wife's birthday. Irma (a key feature of the dream) was present in the dream. Already Freud is asserting a wish fulfilment within his interpretation by the word 'anticipation' (Pp. 108). Freud then demonstrates the use of displacement as he states that the *'responsibility'* for the recorded pains Irma had complained in the dream were not his responsibility (Pp. 109). Also, a noticeable difference had been noted of Irma's appearance. Freud then suspects that *'someone else was being substituted for her'* (Pp.109). In accordance with Freud's analysis this would resemble the process of condensation, in at least so far as to place the question with whom or what is really being represented.

The schematic picture of the psychical apparatus

The transformation from day-dreams to dreams is a process of transforming thoughts into sensory images. The dream state then enables the attachment of belief which in turn strengthens the dream to appear as a real experience.

Within the psychical apparatus lies a sensory end and a motor end. In the sensory end the system receives perceptions. In the motor end the system opens the gateway to motor activity. The current from which the psychical processes naturally flow is from the perceptual end to the motor end. Freud resembles the construction of the psychical apparatus to that of a reflex apparatus, *'Reflex processes remain the model of every psychical function',* (Freud 1901 Pp. 538).

The function of the apparatus is to process a perceptual stimulus which then transforms the momentary excitations into permanent traces. There are two systems at work here. The first system is identified as the preconscious located at the motor end. Processes that excite this part of the system have direct entry into consciousness, however, this is dependent on the level of intensity. The second system is identified as the unconscious and this lies directly behind the first system, because it has *'no access to consciousness except via the preconscious, in passing through which its excitatory process is obliged to submit modifications',* (Freud 1901 Pp. 541).

Freud then notes that the starting point of the dream formation is located within the unconscious. Freud asserts that the construction of a dream is mostly located in the second system, that of the 'unconscious'. This is correct according to the formation of a dream-wish. However, not entirely of the construction of a dream, as thoughts influenced by the preconscious system can attach themselves to the forming of dream thoughts with the intention of gaining access to consciousness.

The excitation which is experienced within a hallucinatory dream moves in a backward direction, towards the sensory end instead of the motor end of the apparatus, finally reaching the perceptual system. This demonstrates that dreams are very much regressive as opposed to progressive which is attributed to the direction that is taken by psychical processes arising from the unconscious during waking life.

According to this theory, dreams should demonstrate that they are influenced by implicit memories which are subject to repression. Also, memory traces that are only accessed during sleep bare an influence upon the individual. Although much of the material that is processed within dreams is under a certain line of repression they will have a direct influence also on the individual's emotional state.

Wish-fulfilment

Freud in 1900 had developed and was continually revising the idea that dreams were/are wish-fulfilments, satisfying in the unconscious dream state what can not be satisfied in reality. However, according to Freud daydreams too play a vital part in the formation of dreams as they are the waking analogue of the process. This sheds light on the very possibility that the unconscious is affected throughout the day via conscious processes that precede it, and this in turn determines what is dreamt. According to Haffner (1887) dreams are a continuation of the waking life. They attach on to thoughts from that of the conscious. Through accurate observation of the dream Haffner imbues that a connection to the previous day is identified, *'a thread which connects the dream to experience'*. Freud qualifies this by stating that, *"no dream is prompted by motives other than egoistic ones"* (Freud 1901 Pp. 664).

According to Feud dreams are formed by the id, the id is governed by the pleasure/un-pleasure principle, and therefore, dreams exhibit an expression of a wish-fulfilment that stems from the unconscious psychical apparatus. In which case the ego can not overpower this process or interfere as it would during the waking stage as the ego is weakened whilst in an unconscious state.

An interesting point to be raised here is that if dreams contain material that is unconsciously processed and expressed during the unconscious state, it can then be suggested that dreams therefore contain direct access to the understanding of unconscious behavioural intensions; *'The interpretation of dreams is the royal road to a knowledge of the unconscious activities of the mind'*, (Freud 1901 Pp. 608). This implies that the process of interpreting dreams will demonstrate a wealth of knowledge about the individual and this is an essential part of Psychoanalysis.

Freud is adamant that there is a psychological technique which makes it possible to interpret dreams (Freud 1900 Pp. 1). He then asserts that a psychical structure is employed which has a meaning. This should be carefully placed at an assignable point when recalling of the dream.

Freud notes four possible origins for such a wish (Freud 1901 Pp. 551). The first, arousal during the day of external reasons that have not brought about any satisfaction are then, in turn, to be dealt with at night via the unconscious. The second, a cause of suppressed material such as a wish that may have arisen during the day, not being fully satisfied, hence, repudiated. The third possible origin for a wish is what Freud exhibits mostly in children the wishful stimulated impulses that arise when asleep of sexual needs or thirst, as Freud states, *'The thirst gives rise to a wish to drink, and the dream shows me that wish fulfilled'* (Freud

1900 Pp. 123). Lastly, the fourth origin for a wish may emerge from the suppressed part of the mind, in this case not the preceding day but material that lay dormant or suppressed and becomes active in sleep mode. This kind of origin for a wish is then explained by Freud stemming from infantile suppression. An example, of this can be located in Appendix A, A premonitory dream fulfilled, (Freud 1901 Pp. 623-625). FRAU B. had reported that a few years ago she had dreamt of meeting Dr. K. in a popular shopping street in the centre of Vienna in front of Heiss shop. The next morning she had met the Dr. K. in the very same place of her dream. At face validity this all seems very prophetic and can without analysis yield as a miraculous rendezvous. However, it was later discovered that it was quite possible that FRAU B. constructed a false connection, the claim of the dream, which stems from her emotional state of mind. The very fact that there is indeed an account of an emotional connection between FRAU B. and Dr. K., '…..*he made love to the woman and for the first and last time set her passion aflame'*, suggests that it is entirely possible that FRAU B. could have been ready at any time for an encounter with Dr. K. This is edified as the passage continues. It is also noted that FRAU B. gives a real account of a time when she was unhappy, being in a room, kneeling, longing for her friend, the very next moment in he comes to visit her, Dr. K. It is clear that FRAU B is exhibiting the effect of being in love and harbouring emotional attachments of thoughts. The occasion of meeting Dr. K. the next morning at the place of her acclaimed dream was, as evidence should suggest, a wish-fulfilment that her unconscious had determined. It is possible that suppression stemming back many years can influence unconscious thoughts and bring dreams to reality.

By the implication of an emotional attachment being present, this strengthens Freud's notion on the libido, there is clearly a sexual intention that FRAU B. harbours towards Dr. K. This account clearly demonstrates that FRAU B. is consciously continually processing thoughts towards Dr. K., and the unconscious naturally threads the material together. It is a working progress of an infusion of suppressed material and conscious expectation.

According to the schematic picture of the psychical apparatus the origin of the first kind of wish is a localization of wishes that pertain to the system of the preconscious. The second kind exhibit a filtering process from the preconscious into the unconscious, and the third kind of wishful impulse originates and stems from the conscious, however, if the dream is not reinforced by the unconscious awakening a wish then the dream will not materialise (Freud 1901 Pp. 553). This kind of origin for a wish resembles the first kind in that the process according to the schematic picture of the psychical apparatus is localised in the preconscious. The fourth kind are unable to escape the unconscious, presumably they are stationed in the unconscious.

A Problem of the theory of dreams as wish-fulfilments

Freud identifies a difficulty with his theory of dreams as wish-fulfilments and this is noted within the New Introductory Lectures (Freud 1932 Pp. 57-58). People that have experienced a traumatic event, such as a war, can be taken back into that traumatic situation when they are dreaming. Why does this happen? This should not happen according to Freud's hypothesis of the function of dreams. However, the answer may lie in suppressed material that lay dormant and is active whilst asleep (Freud 1901 Pp. 551). According to the schematic picture of the psychical apparatus the unconscious will harbour what seemingly are traumatic thoughts and inter-relate them with thoughts of childhood emotion.

A very famous case that demonstrates this sort of problem is the dream of the burning child, *'the father had a dream that his child was standing beside his bed, caught him by the arm and whispered to him reproachfully: 'Father, don't you see I'm burning?'* (Freud 1900 Pp. 509). In reality the child had died and was laid on the bed with candles around him next door to his father. One might say that this was a prophetic dream because the child was really burning in the next room due to a fallen candle that lit the clothing of the child. However, Freud's explanation includes an external element that whilst the father was sleeping a glare from the next room (his son's room) prompted the dream to commence, *'The father drew this inference in a dream instead of allowing himself to be woken up by the glare'* (Freud 1901 Pp. 571). Freud goes onto suggest that the father's dream could be a wish to see his son alive, even if it is only for a brief moment.

Even though Freud asserts a wish-fulfilment within this dream, there is nevertheless a question of trauma that leads to anxiety. Freud develops a theory that accommodates his interpretation. The dream clearly demonstrates a question of self torture; even though a wish-fulfilment has been exhibited there is still a question of traumatic pain. According to 'beyond the pleasure principle' (Freud 1920), Freud introduces the theory of repetition compulsion to explain that when a sudden traumatic experience is repeated by the patient the anxiety that prepares the patient for danger could be built up and dealt with in retrospect (Berry, R., 2000 Pp. 65). Punishment dreams, in this light, *'merely replace the forbidden wish-fulfilment by the appropriate punishment for it; that is to say, they fulfil the wish of the sense of guilt which is the reaction to the repudiated impulse'* (Freud 1920 Pp. 32).

Freud's notion on compulsion repetition is expressed through children's play as he had observed with one particular case. A child of one and a half presented a game formularised by the very essence of his mother leaving him for a few hours, then returning. Freud notes that the child would throw things out of sight and then find them again after a few moments. The initial action is distressing, that the object that belonged to the child would be out of sight, just like his mother, however, once recovered an element of joy would be expressed within the child, just like with his mothers return (Freud 1920 Pp. 14-15). The game is an attempt to parallel the emotion that the child feels when his mother leaves him and when she returns. The child had developed a compulsion repetition that demonstrates distressing activity which follows a rewarding ending.

In this light what more could be said of the burning child dream? It is quite possible that the father had constructed a dream that would punish him in order to feel the relief when he awoke. On one side of the spectrum his son is alive within the dream speaking to him and that is within itself a wish-fulfilment. However, the child is burning and the words spoken are in the nature of a distressing question, *'Father, don't you see I'm burning?'* (Freud 1901 Pp. 509). The reward is the father waking from the dream, a reduction of anxiety and tension is the aim.

This leads Freud to formularise what is known as the death instinct, *'the aim of life is death'* (Freud 1920 Pp. 38). The connection is made on the premise that behaviour is focused at reducing tension and gaining a previously existing state of stability.

Finale

It is apparent that dreams do function as a wish-fulfilment through the psychoanalytical evidence collated. This is best exhibited by children's dreams as this theory is put in a simplistic way, for example, the child's wish-fulfilment of drinking water (Freud 1900 Pp. 123), or eating a type of food (Freud 1900 Pp. 267-268). As the child gets older the amount of complexities that accommodate dreaming also widen. The wish fulfilment may not be so obvious and becomes ever more increasingly difficult to locate. However, with the right methodological technique of interpretation, understanding and asserting the key tools, such as, displacement and condensation, by understanding the individual's intentions of behaviour and relations with others, and with an insight of the individuals' history, it is possible to identify the wish-fulfilment of a complex dream as demonstrated with FRAU B (Freud 1901 Pp. 623-625).

Bibliography

Erdely, M. H. (1985) Psychoanalysis; Freud's cognitive psychology, (1985), W. H. Freeman and Company New York.

Freud, S. (1932) Re-published in 1977, 'New Introductory Lectures on Psychoanalysis', Edited by Richards, A. The Pelican Freud Library, Great Britain.

Freud, S. (1900) Re-published in 2001, 'The Interpretation of Dreams', The Standard edition of the complete psychological works, Edited by Strachey, J. Vintage publications, London.

Freud, S. (1900-1901) Re-published in 2001, 'The Interpretation of Dreams and on Dreams', The Standard edition of the complete psychological works, Edited by Strachey, J. Vintage publications, London.

Freud, S. (1920-1922) Re-published in 2001, 'Beyond the Pleasure Principle', The Standard edition of the complete psychological works of Sigmund Freud, Edited by Strachey, J. Vintage publications, London.

Jones, E. (1961) The Life and Works of Sigmund Freud, Edited by Trilling, L., and Marcus, S. Penguin Books, Great Britain.

Kevin, J., Conner, and Malmin, K. (1983) Interpreting the Scriptures, A text book on how to interpret the Bible, (An introduction to Hermeneutics), Bible Temple Publishing, Portland Oregon, USA.

Kline, P. (1995) Psychology and Freudian theory, An introduction, Routledge, Pp. 77.

Laplanche, J., and Pontalis, J.-B. (2006) The Language of Psychoanalysis, Karnac books, London.

Nelson, T. (1992) 'New King James Version', Holy Bible, 1992, Inc. Republic of Korea.

Theory and Technique: Libido, Oedipus Complex and Neurosis
Jung and Freud's Account

Freud and Jung collaborated between 1906 and 1913, much of their work was attractive to the Psychiatric and Psychological world. Freud was in the process of consolidating the insights developed over the preceding decade and in the process of an international movement. The relationship with Jung helped Freud and assisted with reaching a greater audience as Jung (at the time thirty-one) was a Psychiatrist of a high reputation already working at one of Europe's major centres for treatment of psychotic disorders. This supported Freud in the process of linking Psychoanalysis to the international reputation of the Burghölzli Psychiatric Clinic with the support of a Professor of Psychiatry in Zurich namely Eugen Bleuler. In 1904 Bleuler had liaised with Freud and expressed his keen attempts of applying psychoanalysis and finding various forms of it which would support Freud's theories via the experimental method of psychology (Jones, E. 1981 Pp. 326). However, the main contribution came from Carl Jung (Bleuler's chief assistant at that) in his studies of word association, with a list of 100 words read out to the participant s/he is then asked to respond systematically to each and every word that comes into his or hers head. This demonstrates a correlation between stimulus and response that participants are influenced by words that arouse emotion and therefore slow down their response (Storr, A. 1998). This strengthened Freud's psychoanalytic practice as it sheds light on emotional thought processes that are cued by certain words. The relationship with Freud allowed Jung to broaden his perspective on the etiology and treatment of both neurosis and psychosis, as both men collaborated, and by this he became more active within the international psychoanalytic movement.

The very reason why Psychoanalysis was introduced was as a response to human suffering. Therefore, it is absolutely crucial that the practice of therapy would meet the patient's needs as much as well a clearer understanding of human behaviour.

Freud and Jung eventually parted ways (physically at least) in 1912 due to various differences in theory and technique. To gain some understanding of these differences it is important to note how each man viewed the patient, as this would indicate and clearly demonstrate that the psychological techniques employed by both men had differed.

One of the main reasons why both men split off into different directions was on the notion of the libido. Freud's theory of the libido is hypothesized as mental energy which derives from the id and is mostly sexual in nature (Reber, A 1995 Pp. 418). It is further elaborated to include underlying *'the transformations of the sexual drive with respect to its object, (displacement of cathexes), with respect to its aim (e.g. sublimation), and with respect to the source of sexual excitation (diversity of the erotogenic zones')*, (Laplanche, J., and Pontalis, J.-B. 2006 Pp. 239).

Jung's contribution and interpretation of the libido was as a theory of 'psychic energy' (Storr, A. 1998). In May 1911 Jung expressed to Freud that he regarded the libido merely as a designation of general tension. Jung's work on this topic can be found in his essay on 'Symbols of the libido', which is put together in two parts. It is within the second part of the essay that his differences from Freud's theory were expressed, and in November later that year Jung announced his plans to demonstrate a broader understanding of the libido.

According to Jung the dynamics of the libido are very much in the concept of a psychic energy that include a continual satisfaction of the demands of the environmental condition (CW 8 Pp. 60-69). For progression to occur it is essential that the Patient acknowledges the need to satisfy the demands of adaptation via a suitable directed attitude. Accordingly, Jung asserts that a two step process is needed in order for a clearer understanding of the Patient's psychic mental attitude, (1) attainment of attitude, (2) completion of adaptation by means of the attitude (Storr, A. 1998 Pp. 59). However, the attitude can no longer satisfy adaptation if changes occur in the environment that requires a different attitude. This will bring on an in-balance and therefore cause an irregularity of psychic energy that will slow down the progression of the libido. Therefore, it is apparent to Jung that there is a continual effort made in harmonizing and a balancing of the two sides of attitude and adaptation to environment. Jung (1921) notes that the environment has an impact on development and hypothesizes a process of cognitive preferences that are innate in construction but environmentally influenced (Segal, M. 2001 Pp. 57).

For Jung a great deal of emphasis is placed on the patient's need to become this whole self-being. This concept of 'the whole' would mean the bringing together of the contradictory and irreconcilable aspects of his or hers total self.

According to Jung the slowing down of the libido is the unbalancing of 'psychic energies' and therefore the Patient could prospectively develop neurotic symptoms. *'At its heart, the neurosis is understood by Jung as part of the individuals struggle to reconcile the apparently contradictory, opposing aspects of himself'* (Barton, A. 1974 Pp. 92).

The year 1911 continued to see both men through many of their differences and the problems raised by their conflict over the boundaries of meaning. Jung during this time questioned the problem of the loss of reality with a personal observation on Freud:

Jung wrote to Freud, December 1911:

> *The loss of the reality function in D.pr. cannot be reduced to repression of libido (defined as sexual hunger). Not by me at any rate. Your doubt shows me that in your eyes as well the problem cannot be solved this way.* (Freud/Jung Letters Pp. 471)

Jung continued within the same letter to address a problem with Freud's notion on the Libido asserting the need for a biological explanation:

> *The essential point is that I try to replace the descriptive concept of the libido by a genetic one. Such a concept covers not only the recent-sexual libido but all those forms of it which have long since split off into organized activities. A wee bit of biology is unavoidable here.* (Freud/Jung Letters Pp. 471)

Freud's notion of the libido was not dependent on biology, as he had already demonstrated in a letter to Jung 30 November 1911:

> *What troubles me most is that Fraulein Spierlrein wants to subordinate the psychological material to biological considerations; this dependency is no more acceptable than a dependency on philosophy, physiology, or brain anatomy.* (Freud/Jung Letters Pp. 469)

Freud made it clear that Psychoanalysis does not have to justify itself within the existing sciences of the anatomy of human biology, and why would it need to? Freud's account of the libido is more in line with evolutionary psychology (psychological explanation of the evolution of human behaviour and existence) and this can be demonstrated by employing more modern scientific observation to the study and practice of Psychoanalysis, as shall be demonstrated later. However, what is interesting here is that Jung continued to question Freud about the functioning of the libido and regarded Freud's notion of it as *'doubtful'* (Freud/Jung Letters 1911 Letters Pp. 471). Perhaps it was Jung who doubted Freud's concept of the libido and projected his fears about this onto Freud hoping to get a reaction in order to revise the theory of the libido.

The libido is more than just an explanation of *'energy postulated as underlying the transformations of sexual instinct with respect to its object (displacement of cathexes)'* (Laplanche, J., and Pontalis, J.-B. 2006 Pp. 239). Freud is so close to the evolutionary psychological theory of survival and reproduction, for this to be demonstrated the question asked should be of its theory of function, presuming that human behaviour is governed by certain laws of nature. Freud postulates that the Oedipus complex explains the structuring of human beings as sexual beings and during this *'the complex's effects on the structuring of personality – on the constitution of the different agencies, particularly the super-ego and the ego-ideal'*, (Laplanche, J., and Pontalis, J.-B. 2006 Pp. 285)

Furthermore, a clear example that can stem as a product of the libido for some people (if not all people) would be in the form of a neurosis. This leads as a consequence if society on the whole are sexually charged with sexual impulses governing their behaviour and the Oedipus complex according to Freud (1920) is therefore the Signifier of Culture. In this respect it can be further imbued that within the construction of sexuality there also lies the construction of personality and soon the construction of cultural and social development. *'It has justly been said that the Oedipus complex is the nuclear complex of the neuroses, and constitutes the essential part of their content. It represents the peak of infantile sexuality, which, through its after-effects, exercises a decisive influence on the sexuality of adults. Every new arrival on this planet is faced by the task of mastering the Oedipus complex; anyone who fails to do so falls a victim to neurosis.'* (Freud 1905 Pp. 226)

This statement has two important implications, firstly, that neurosis is as a consequence of not fully mastering the Oedipus complex. This is demonstrated by employing the prohibition against incest. In Freud's terms this is a natural satisfaction process where a link between wish and law is sought in order to, in sum, preserve civilization. Secondly, the importance of the Oedipus complex is highlighted within Psychoanalysis, indicating that Psychoanalysis was becoming refined around this theory.

When determining the interpretation of the libido that leads to neurosis, a critical question to ask is; what is its theory of function and what purpose does it serve? This is to measure each theory of Freud's and Jung's according to a more accurate evolutionary process that governs the principles of behaviour.

Initially Freud developed his practice investigating main areas of human thought and behaviour. However, Freud specifically identified neurosis as a major component for further investigation. It is important to note that in Freud's notion of the neurotic patient exists repression, which includes an incompatibility between the person's ideals and impulses that are continually emerging. This is of crucial importance as when compared to Jung's account and history of repression. For Freud, ideals were of such a nature that merited the patient with high self expectation and vulnerability to symptoms such as anxiety and depression due to disappointment. A major part of repression is processed through, as Freud would put it, semi-conscious and semi-unconscious processes. However, according to Freud, an unconscious impulse which arises will always stem from conflicts related to sexuality. This then would lead to a neurosis. It can be further argued that the unconscious would be chiefly responsible for construction of the neurosis as the 'id' is located there and therefore it manifests itself as an impulse. The conscious part of the mind is in a continual struggle to adhere to the moral set of standards and therefore via the ego suppresses material that, interestingly enough, conflicts with its values and trends. This has a great bearing on the patient and can potentially lead the patient to develop false-connections due to misunderstood and misinterpreted material that has been presented to the conscious state of the mind. An example of this is made clear as Freud notes when dealing with Frau P.J. a lady aged twenty-six whom longs for her husband, *'that is, for sexual relations with him; she had thus come upon an idea which had excited sexual affect and afterwards defence against the idea; she had then taken fright and made a false connection or substitution'* (Freud 1886 Pp. 216).

There is clearly a workable theory of function that Freud had demonstrated, within his practice and account of neurosis, which can be further elaborated to include an evolutionary system of process. It is within the framework of an evolutionary system of process that Freud's notion on neurosis can be fully appreciated and to some degree acknowledged as a mechanical science of behaviour. The indication is quite clear, Freud's notion on neurosis could possibly serve a purpose.

According to Bernard and Brisset Manual de Psychiatrie (1963) *'By neurotic systems. These are disturbances of behaviour, of the emotions or of thought which make manifest a defense against anxiety and constitute a compromise in respect of this internal conflict from which the subject, in his neurotic position, derives a certain advantage'* (secondary gain from neurosis). It is with this secondary gain that a proposal of a theory of function can be exhibited, remembering of course, that Freud alludes neurosis to conflicts related to sexuality, therefore it can further be imbued that the process adheres to pleasure seeking of the body, in turn, unconsciously processing material that influences behaviour and is suppressed by the ego. It is here that the patient is a victim of misinterpreting material that is consciously processed and forms false-connections.

In the three essays on the theory of sexuality Freud asserts that the Libido is not much different from sexual desire in search of satisfaction (Freud 1905 Pp.217). The libido in this sense is the mechanism for which the sexual drive is illustrated. An impressive discovery of Freud's day, of which an undertone of reproduction is slowly creeping in. The indication for reproduction here would be alluding to a sexual urge for satisfaction, as such an impulse would be the root of such a cause.

To further demonstrate that Freud is very close to the mark of understanding and dissecting neurosis as a manifestation of infantile sexual conflicts arising as impulses, it would be necessary to take into account a 'reductionism' perspective and turn to evolutionary psychology to fully appreciate Freud's notion on the Libido and how it is in connection to neurosis.

According to Richard Dawkins 'the selfish gene' (1976) the need to reproduce and persevere one's genes is the sole basis of every living organism in existence. Therefore, it would be right to assert that a sexual impulse is present within the human make-up (after all, this is purpose driven). This directs our attention to the level of the gene and its importance of function, *'A gene is defined as any portion of chromosomal material that potentially lasts for enough generations to serve as a unit of natural selection'* (Pp. 28). Dawkins continues to elaborate on this theme with his main target to assign a functional purpose on the genome level. In the simplest of ways *'the true 'purpose' of DNA is to survive, no more and no less'* (Pp. 45). By the DNA encoding a sexual impulse into human beings this need to survive is assured, as where the need within the individual is strong enough then reproduction will occur.

Crawford (1993) points out that the impulse for sex stems from neural hardware selected for the constructing-information processing mechanisms, which then leads to current human behaviour (Cartwright, J. 2000 Pp. 47). In this light there is a relationship between ancestral adaptations and current human behaviour, implying that sexual impulses are indeed an influence on human behaviour.

There seems to be a link with Freud's theory of the Libido and the genetic sexual theory of reproduction. However, it is important to clarify that Freud demonstrated his theory of the libido not for the sole purpose of reproduction, but to indicate an existent sexual impulse that is present in every human being that in turn influences behaviour: *'To begin with, sexual activity attaches itself to functions serving the purpose of self-preservation and does not become independent of them until later'* (1905 Pp. 182). To appreciate this further it would be necessary to revert back to Freud's notion on neurosis. This can now be defined as the defense and product of the ego suppressing the urge for sexual satisfaction, and is made evident by hysteria. One might further say, to protect society and its moral standards.

In Freud's account of the libido there is clearly a workable theory that encompasses the whole of the individual and social network. To reiterate, the libido includes the individual's sexual instinct which is expressed by impulses that carry the individual through life with the intention of self-preservation and self-satisfaction that also unite *'human beings through an ever – increasing reinforcement of the sense of guilt'* (Freud 1931 Pp. 133). In turn, through the structure of sexuality via the Oedipal process the individual is then constructed within society that stems from infantile turn taking, an expression that demonstrates the instinct of sexual interaction of the infant and the object, *'The child's lips, in our view, behave like an erotogenic zone, and no doubt stimulation by the warm flow of milk is the cause of the pleasurable sensation. The satisfaction of the erotogenic zone is associated, in the first instance, with the satisfaction of the need for nourishment'* (Freud 1905 Pp. 181-182).

Jung embraces a very much different concept that explains the functioning of the libido. He believes that the libido extends beyond sexual impulses and addresses other areas of life, he introduces a concept that explains 'energy' leading to desire, Jung continues to call this new process 'libido, in its true form'. In this case the energy (libido) in an infant is an instinct pertaining to nutritional needs, not sexual (as Freud would put it). Jung further explains that the child gains pleasure in sucking – converted as pleasure in nutrition.

However, although Jung's foundation of the libido is different than that of Freud's, he asserts that the lead up to neurosis could possibly be a valuable signal which would indicate, a false set of values or an evasion of responsibilities; a derailment of an individual from his true path. Neurotic symptoms then, would serve to compensate a self-regulating system in order for a better balance within the psyche. 'Balance' is the key in order to understand Jung's intentions within his notion of neurosis. He places great emphasis on a theory of function for neurosis and that the neurotic patient is in some ways at an advantage. Now the patient can draw attention to psychological problems which are not made evident and that they are unaware of.

Mark and Nesse (1994) have contributed an immense amount of research on the topic of nervous conditional strategies that contribute to survival and that of reproduction. They hypothesize that nervous conditions and those that lead to anxiety disorders serve a purpose in that anxiety increases fitness in dangerous situations which threaten a loss of reproductive resources. This indirectly supports Jung's notion on neurosis as serving a purpose in respect to the preservation of life and not being classed as an illness of disabilitating effect. However, notice also how this research on nervousness also is directed to include reproduction as its aim, then asserting the nervous condition as its tool.

Through both concepts of the libido, that of Freud's and that of Jung's, it would only be right to highlight that Freud's concept closely hits the mark of an explanation that acknowledges a theory of sexual importance that extends to the construction of society as well as that of the individual and the self. However, as demonstrated, it can be argued that Freud's theory addresses the very rudimentary level of human behaviour and could even be touching upon the genome level, perhaps without intending to. There is more evidence to suggest that Freud's theory of the libido is more in line with evolutionary processes of adaptation and survival than Jung's account, and this is due to the very notion of sexual impulses that govern and influence the individual in how s/he acts in the world. Freud's theory is being made more accurate through modern day evolutionary psychological research, there is certainly a foundation to start with. However, even though Jung's theory of the processes of the libido may not be as evolutionary psychologically accurate as Freud's in following the same principals of the evolutionary laws that govern life in reproduction and survival, it has nevertheless a unique explanation for neurosis that serves a purpose and could possibly be in line as an evolutionary explanation for its symptoms. Jung's theory of the libido embraces 'psychical energy' in general which should not be dismissed, as it holds technical value within human behaviour in general.

Bibliography

Barton, A. (1974) Three Worlds of Therapy, An Extential-Phenomenological Study of the Therapies of Freud, Jung, and Rogers, Duquesne University, Mayfield Publishing Company.

Cartwright, J. (2000) Evolution and Human Behaviour, Darwinian Perspectives on Human Nature, Palgrave.

Dawkins, R. (1976) The Selfish Gene, Oxford University Press, Great Britain.

Freud, S. (1886-1899) Re-published 2001 'Extracts from the Fliess Papers', The Standard Edition of the Complete Psychological Works. Strachey, J., ed., in collaboration with Freud, A., Volume one, Vintage Publications.

Freud, S. (1901-1905) Re-published 2001 'Infantile Sexuality'. The Standard Edition of the Complete Psychological Works. Strachey, J., ed., in collaboration with Freud, A., Volume seven, Vintage publications.

Freud, S. (1901-1905) Re-published 2001 'Jokes and their Relation to the Unconscious'. The Standard Edition of the Complete Psychological Works. Strachey, J., ed., in collaboration with Freud, A., Volume Eight, Vintage publications.

Freud, S. (1927-1931) Re-published 2001 'Civilization and its Discontents'. The Standard Edition of the Complete Psychological Works. Strachey, J. ed., in collaboration with Anna Freud., Volume twenty-one, Vintage publications.

Hogenson, G.B. (1983) Jung's Struggle With Freud, University of Notre Dame Press.

Jung, C. (1916-1928) 'Psychoanalysis and Neurosis' and 'On Psychic Energy'. The Essential Jung, Selected Writings Introduced by Storr, A., 1998, Fontana Press, London.

Laplanche, J., and Pontalis, J.-B. (2006) The Language of Psychoanalysis, Karnac books, London.

Marks and Nesse (1994) Fear and Fitness: An Evolutionary Analysis of Anxiety Disorders, Journal of Evolutionary Psychology.

McGuire, W. ed., (1974) The Freud/Jung Letters. Translated by Manheim, R., and Hull, R.F.C., The Hogarth Press and Routledge and Kegan Paul, London, Pp. 471.

Segal, M. (2001) 'Carl Jung's Theory of Personality', Creativity and Personality Type, Tools for Understanding and Inspiring, The Many Voices of Creativity, Telos Publications, California, USA.

Winnicott's Theory of Development:
Understanding Play as Constructing the Child's Personal World

In order to appreciate the psychodynamic approach of the theory of development, one needs a cohesive account as to what prolongs the child's understanding in his or hers discursive account of object identification in relation to the self. Winnicott lends favour to a theory that amplifies 'BEING' in order to 'DO'. According to Winnicott 'BEING' is a state that comes about as *'a result of the infant's subjective experience of being merged with a good-enough mother,'* (Abram, J. 1996 Pp. 57). From this pivotal point the infant can then create and construct the world that he or she lives in and from this experience the infant can achieve a sense of 'BEING' that is real.

D. W. Winnicott was born in 1896 and died in 1971 just after compiling a collection of essays that would soon be known as the book 'Playing and Reality'. He was an admirable theorist as well as a psychoanalyst as he influenced much of the current topics in psychoanalysis in his day. This was reflected in his status as President of the British Psycho-Analytical Society and President of the Paediatric Section of the Royal Society of Medicine.

Winnicott tailored a theory of child development that has its roots in the in-between stages of 'practice' and play (Gouldman, D. 1993 Pp. xii). According to Winnicott playing is a vital part of development that shares its qualities with discovery. Playing in this sense never ceases to diminish as the child grows older. Winnicott states that play can also be observed between the psychotherapist and the patient and this demonstrates a healthy communicative system between the two (Winnicott 1971 Pp. 51 & 64).

However, although playing is customary to Winnicott's theory, one may include 'practice' as the cause of play. In this view the child seeks the best possible way that he or she can manipulate the environment in order to gain the most creative encounter and acceptance. It is through practice that the child can be most effective when playing, and it is essential to the child's basic form of living as it is always a creative experience (Winnicott 1971 Pp. 67). The child works on an object that he or she is attracted to and places an 'I' within the scheme of playing. The child then rehearses or role plays in order to achieve a certain level of understanding to support his or her efforts in social bonding. Although alone during the rehearsal process the child needs to *'live through a deep personal experience in order to arrive at the understanding'* (Winnicott 1971 Pp. 99). So in this way the child 'practices' play intending to construct the world to that which the child belongs. This is only achieved within the child's privacy as he will have his whole life to play, 'practice' therefore is vital for development. Winnicott connects infantile experience with sophisticated cultural production. His theory of play suggests that there is a space between object and interpretation, an 'intermediate zone' which is separate yet interlinked. This space was adjacent to, and drew its energy from, what Winnicott had termed "primary psychic creativity" (Caldwell 2000 Pp. 15). This is a unique perspective that has potential to offer insight on child development and a new line within psychoanalytic thought.

The attractive object which the child is drawn to is a construction of what the child perceives to be the missing comfort of his life. Winnicott elaborates that the mother's breast constructs for the infant an emotional tie that is blueprinted within the child's unconscious and expresses itself in the form of an object relating to the emotional thought pattern that is associated with the child's first love object and soon to become incorporated within the infant's environment. However, the breast is a lot more significant, as the baby whilst developing his or her identity, becomes the breast (Winnicott 1971 Pp. 107). According to Winnicott the breast is a symbol of being (Winnicott 1971 Pp. 109), it is of 'BEING' that the baby can then 'DO'. It is an essential feature that the construction of identity is based on the child's love object, that to which is a familiar object and therefore, of great value and in this sense the 'transitional object' is introduced.

The transitional object stands for some symbolic-part of the breast (Clancier, A. 1984 Pp. 84) and is the infant's defence against anxiety. In this case the transitional object is a privileged item, for example, a rag, pillow, teddy bear or something similar, to which the infant forms an attachment to in a *'habitual and tyrannical'* way (Clancier, A. & Kalmanovitch 1987 Pp. 81). However, Winnicott derives at this conclusion by first asserting a function to transitional space. He introduces this term from observing babies that from birth use their hands, their fingers and their feet to satisfy oral drives and to find peace. This then leads the babies to activities of a different kind, the formulisation of the transitional object (Clancier, A. & Kalmanovitch 1987 Pp. 81). The infant seeks refuge within this object from a state of unknowing, therefore, interpreting his interaction with the transitional object as a safe place to be. This then allows the child to express his ways onto the transitional object in a free manner that separates his actions from his anxieties. It could be further suggested that within this process the child practices his autonomy onto the object and embraces his liberty to do so. However, if this object gets lost, or changes in form, the child will experience a high amount of anxiety as he has lost more than just the symbolic breast but also his right to practice liberty. Winnicott demonstrates this further by implying *'The transitional object antedates established reality-testing'* (Clancier, A. 1984 Pp. 84). He imbues that the value of the transitional object is held within the child's ability to work on the environment in order to gain a clearer understanding of the 'Self' and how the 'Self' is able to construct a reality from the imaginary. This is a precise indication that for Winnicott 'practice' is chiefly responsible for the child's formation of identification. Playing is then essential in the process of creating, and being creative is essential for the individual's discovery of the Self (Winnicott 1971 Pp. 72), however, not necessarily the construction of identification. Identification is flexibly modified according to expectation and therefore can not (solely) derive meaning from the notion of play. This is why 'practice' is considered to conceive the child's identity with no set pattern of regulation or expectation, the child is free, yet again, to construct reality with his marked mistakes he can rehearse in order to learn.

Play on the other hand is a procedure of interaction that demonstrates the ability to sustain order of knowledge. In this case the infant can manipulate the environment to achieve satisfaction, however, more importantly feeling real through meaningful experiences. Whereas Freud posited emphasis on physical gratification as the primary criterion for satisfaction (Goldman, D. 1993 Pp. xvi), Winnicott placed an immense amount of importance on the notion of creativeness that equates to the 'real experience'. 'Feeling real' is an essential feature that Winnicott (1967) derives to that concludes to suggest that the individual is healthy (Goldman, D. 1993 Pp. xvi). Health is a precise feature of Winnicotts theory that further extends the notion that development is based on 'BEING' and 'DOING'. However, the gel that enables this procedure to strengthen in its systematic sequence lies within creativeness. In this sense, from the imaginary the real exists. So, it can be argued that the real is a product of creativity from the imaginary. The infant comes to 'BE' as a result of his or her discourse with the object; the object being the world.

Where Freud saw psychoanalysis *'as a way of freeing people from illusions, Winnicott emphasized the freedom to create and enjoy illusions'* (Goldman, D. 1993 Pp. xxiii). The importance of sustaining an illusion is a requirement in order to sustain happiness. The infant constructs reality from what is known of the imaginary and placed in sequential order of priority, this way the child seeks refuge in a belief system. This is demonstrated throughout the individual's life, for example, taking shape as a religion or cultural art. Although Freud demonstrates that religious ideas and formations are deeply rooted within an illusion, the fulfilment of wishes (Freud 1927 Pp. 30), Winnicott places a value of safety upon the notion (Winnicott 1967, 1990 Pp. 36). This further asserts that the perception of reality may have its roots in a similar place if the theory of the transitional object is fully appreciated and accepted. The child then seeks to construct the world from the position of trust of what he or she is presented with. Elaborated further, Winnicott here presents his theory of 'the holding environment', which provides a sense of safety and trust that depends upon the reliability of the caretaker and affective communication between the caretaker and the child (Goldman, D. 1993 Pp. xix).

Winnicott's theory of development lays down a firm foundation within the maturational processes that facilitate the child's environment, the mother plays a leading role within the child's 'inner world'. In this view *'Primary maternal preoccupation begins as body involvement during pregnancy but becomes specifically linked in fantasy with an "internal object," which, Winnicott (1960, 1989) implies, is tied to the good-enough mother of the expectant mother's own early infancy'* (Gouldman, D.

1993 Pp. 182). This implies that if the mother's internalised environment is poor, she will have difficulty in sustaining a child in fantasy; this will lead to difficulties in forming a relationship with her baby. So, the mother's own experience is of vital importance that reflects how she will bond with her child. The child need's his mother's attention in order to invest trust as the mother will prove to be a key concept to the child's ability to feel real. Winnicott had delivered a talk to the Nursery School Association of Great Britain entitled "The Ordinary Devoted Mother", which he attempted to explain the logic of this notion:

> *There is nothing mystical about this. After all, she was a baby once, and she has in her the memories of being a baby; she also has memories of being cared for, and these memories can either help or hinder her in her own experiences as a mother. [Pp. 6].* (Gouldman, D. 1993 Pp. 183).

What is believed is that the mother can attend to the baby's needs as she was once a baby and from her unconscious recollection she knows that the baby will experience anxiety. Winnicott fundamentally believed that the infant at its earliest stage of development is *'an immature being living a precarious existence on the brink of unthinkable anxieties'* (Gouldman, D. 1993 Pp. 162). At this stage the mother takes centre role in reducing the child's inner conflict by being sensitive to her infant's inner prompting (Gouldman, D. 1993 Pp. 163).

The infant expresses himself in a desperate way knowing that his needs will be met. However, in this case "desperate" does not mean seeking to achieve by being impatient, but as the infant is *'on the brink of unthinkable anxiety'* (Winnicott 1962 Pp. 57) he has no other way to express his desire to create in order to exist. This is a little more then existing to satisfy one's needs but to be satisfied in 'becoming'. It is at this point that the all important 'BE' has its domain to realise the potential to 'DO'. The id impulses are set from the construction of the infant's ability to exercise thought. The id-functioning is collected together in all its aspects and becomes ego-experience. Only then can the infant rely on his mental structures that enable him to trust his ego-experience. In this way the anxiety that the infant has been accustomed to since the beginning of his life is repressed to the level of the unconscious constructing the id. Here the unconscious is a dominant feature throughout the individual's life with the id influencing later life development and function. However, there is no id before ego (Winnicott 1962 Pp. 57) and this can suggest that the id is formulated as a result of the infant suppressing material which is unbearable to live with were it conscious. It is within this process that Winnicott takes a further step into the theoretical assumption that the object (being the world) is the apparatus that the infant manipulates to gain understanding of the self. The emphasis on development at this stage is placed on the infant's ability to love. This indicates how much trust the infant can place on the object to vindicate his identity. Love is of critical importance within this paradigm, as Winnicott states, *"true object love was a developmental achievement of a loving self"* (Gouldman, D. 1993 Pp. 171). By Winnicottian definition the 'loving self' is a 'healthy self' that has achieved his or her creative sense of 'the real', *'Creativity is the doing that arises out of being'* (Winnicott 1986 Pp. 39). The being has arrived and is real to the sustainable illusion of what the object presents. What the object presents is how the individual defines it, the infant creates the object, but the object was there waiting to be created and to become a cathected object (Winnicott 1971 Pp. 119).

The infant's understanding is regulated upon what was first the love object and he has now defined the world that he exists in accordance to his ability to create and identify the self. Depending upon the infants feeling of the real, the sense of having an identity will positively correlate (Winnicott 1971 Pp. 107). This enables the child to develop object love and, again, find himself. Freud's notion on narcissism is considered here as it too is formulated on the assumption that the individual invests love into the object.

Freud's theory of narcissism was first introduced by Freud in 1910 to account for object-choice in homosexuals. However, this discovery leads Freud (1911) in the Schreber case *'to posit the existence of a stage in sexual development between auto-erotism and object love'* (Laplanche, J. and Pontalis, J-B., 2006 Pp. 255). The love-object is first recognised by the infant as his own body, which then leads onto the first unification of the sexual instincts. Freud further expands that from the beginning of mental life; the ego is cathected with instincts and is to some extent capable of satisfying them on itself (Freud 1915 Pp. 134). As the infant's needs are met by the caretaker, the infant has no need to believe that there is an outside world. According to Winnicott (1962) integration emerges out of the 'stuff of primary narcissism' (Gouldman, D. 1993 Pp. 177). This idea of integration can be linked to Freud's notions on primary narcissism. For the infant there is an omnipresent force attending to his vital needs. According to Smith (1985) Narcissism is based on the illusion of self-generated pleasure, dependent, in actuality, on the caretaker's ministrations (Gouldman, D. 1993 Pp. 181). This implicates that the infant is destined to disappointment, and is forced to recognise his own needs and furthermore construct a world that meets them. However, the infant has a blueprint of what he knows as an essential feature to his existence and this is a critical point within Winnicott's theory of development and function, the infant has an unconscious desire of the love-object as he turns his attention onto the world.

A feature that one could add at this point is that the infant never really acknowledges having evolved and having adapted outside his constructed known world for the reason that the world is an extension of his imaginary real. While the id is working on the object and re-defining its use of gratification, the ego defines its boundary. This could be an interpretation of what it is to create. Once the infant invests enough love (trust) within the object the infant can then learn to 'BE'. New meaning then can be asserted to the function of the transitional object, it now provides a safety-net of familiarity, and something that the infant can run back to if he is experiencing high anxiety through failing to integrate. This may be why the transitional object remains with the child almost all the time.

It is through the process of integration that the baby is led to a state of unity, *'to the personal pronoun "I", to the number one; it makes possible the "I am" that gives a sense to "I do"'* (Clancier, A. & Kalmanovitch, J. 1987 Pp. 29). It can be argued that this form of the "I am" is the product of the created sense of self, and only through 'BEING' is this achieved. The infant needs to 'BE' in order to 'DO', and needs to 'DO' in order to facilitate 'BEING', it remains a re-generating process that equates to the "I am" sense of self.

Although Winnicott emphasis the role of the creative being that constructs the real for the infant a connection can be made to the earlier works of Freud as he makes a distinction between two states of the ego, the pleasure-ego and the reality-ego. In this case, the pleasure-ego works in order to yield pleasure and avoiding un-pleasure, the reality-ego strives for what will be useful in guarding itself against damage (Freud 1911 Pp. 223). Here the reality-ego is of particular interest as it is structured within the same concept of Winnicott's notion of creativity. Freud imbues that *'While the ego goes through its transformation from a pleasure-ego into a reality ego, the sexual instincts undergo the changes that lead them from their original auto-erotism through various intermediate phases to object-love in the service of pro-creation'* (Freud 1911 Pp. 224). Although Freud theorises that the infant emerges from a pleasure-ego state to a reality-ego state; a process of metamorphism, Winnicott on the other hand views the infant as a creative being from the start of life striving for the sense of being real, the change that the baby goes through in his theory is one of re-directing object-love, for the intention of constructing a bearable world to live in.

The British Independent School of Psychoanalysis owes much of its development to Donald W. Winnicott. Winnicott has been a key figure within British Psychoanalysis and he has contributed an immense amount of work on the theme of child development. Winnicott considers the child as an inventor of his or her own reality, obtaining knowledge of the world through maternal mental structures which consider the world as an extension of the infant's first primary love-object. He develops a his notion on what it means to 'BE' and how to measure what is real. If taken literally Winnicott's theory of reality can be elaborated to suggest that life is constructed from an imaginary real that one must value, resulting from the created sense of 'BEING'. This then imbues that the infant is free to create an illusion that, as Winnicott believes, should be enjoyed and not discouraged (Gouldman, D. 1993 Pp. xxiii). For Winnicott the illusion is not only put in place as an explanation for religion or even culture but extends to each and every individual's own world that they have created for themselves. The individual has inserted the real within the imaginary and constructed the real from the imaginary. The marked effects of play are of central concern to Winnicott and it is through play that Winnicott can construct his theory of child development with the aid of child observation and interviews, as for example, Winnicot's case of the Piggle. He notes that the child's *'mother has to fall and hurt herself and then Piggle does things to make her better'* (Clancier, A. & Kalmanovitch, J. 1987 Pp. 47). The intention is clear, the child is in a state of play that enables her to love and hate her mother simultaneously. The same way play has been considered as the ability to interact and create; 'practice' should also be considered as a type of rehearsal that enables the child to gain the best possible way to approach play.

Although Winnicott was very much influenced by Freud, the differences between their theory of child development are few but vital. For Freud, accepting and recognising external reality was the baby's central task. He also believed that reality was frustrating from which people never fully recovered. However, for Winnicott, the central task for the baby was to find healthy ways of creating reality and in that reality providing relief and satisfaction from the alarming effects of unrestrained fantasy (Gouldman, D. 1993 Pp. 190).

Finally, as demonstrated Winnicott's theory of primary creativity is one of the most original contributions to psychoanalysis (Gouldman, D. 1993 Pp. 185), and still continues to lead psychoanalytic thought today.

Bibliography

Abram, J. (1996), The Language of Winnicott: a dictionary of Winnicott's use of words, Karnac Books, London.

Cardwell, L. et al, (2000), Art, Creativity, Living, Karnac Books, London and New York.

Clancier, A., and Jeannine, K. (1987), Winnicott and Paradox: from birth to creation, Tavistock Publications, London and New York.

Davis, M., and Wallbridge. D. (1981), Boundary and Space, An Introduction to the Work of D. W. Winnicott, Karnac Books, London.

Freud, S. (1911) Re-printed in 2001, 'Formulations on the Two Principles of Mental Functioning', The Standard Edition of the Complete Psychological Works, Strachey, J. ed., in collaboration with Anna Freud., Volume 12, Re-published by Vintage publications.

Freud, S. (1915) Re-printed in 2001, 'Instincts and their Vicissitudes', The Standard Edition of the Complete Psychological Works, Strachey, J. ed., in collaboration with Anna Freud., Volume 14, Re-published by Vintage publications.

Freud, S. (1927) Re-published 2001 'The Future of an Illusion'. The Standard Edition of the Complete Psychological Works. Strachey, J. ed., in collaboration with Anna Freud., Volume twenty-one, Re-published by Vintage publications.

Gouldman, D. (1993), In Search of the Real: The Origins and Originality of D. W. Winnicott, Jason Aronson Inc. Northvale, New Jersey, London.

Laplanche, J., and Pontalis, J.-B. (2006) The Language of Psychoanalysis, Karnac books, London.

Winnicott, D. W. (1986) Reprinted 1990, Home is Where We Start From, Edited by Winnicott, C., Shepherd, R., and Davis, Madeleine, Penguin Books, London.

Winnicott, D. W. (1977) Reprinted 1991, The Piggle: An Account of the Psychoanalytic Treatment of a Little Girl, Edited by Ramzy, I., Penguin Books, London.

Winnicott, D. W. (1957) Reprinted 1991, The Child, the Family and the Outside World, Penguin Books, London.

Winnicott, D. W. (1971) Reprinted 2005, Playing and Reality, Routledge Classics, London and New York.

Winnicott, D. W. (1965), The Maturational Process and The Facilitating Environment. Studies in the Theory of Emotional Development. The Hogarth Press and the Institute of Psycho-Analysis, London.

Winnicott, D. W. (1962), Ego Integration in Child Development. Studies in the Theory of Emotional Development. The Hogarth Press and the Institute of Psycho-Analysis, London.

Examining 'The Order' of the Group and its Formation

"if it should turn out that life has no purpose, it would lose all value for them"
(Freud 1927 Pp. 75)

Important note:
*(Before reading this paper I must clarify two most important points that without clarification could be misleading. Firstly, the ideal 'illusion' as commented within this essay relates to a principle that is constructed with the view of **being attained**. In other words, an illusion does not necessarily allude to an imaginary construction of reality that is not attainable. Secondly, group formation such as the 'Assembly' is expanded upon with the intention to examine the underlying current of social affairs and the need to cultivate the groups' belief in a system. Identifying this on an unconscious level only strengthens the notion of group formation for purpose, in which case leaves room for theological questioning. This contributes to the common need for a collective interest in the ideal 'illusion', which according to law and custom may be achievable through faith in the system and its order. This is the only place where I reserve my belief in that not all ideal 'illusions' are not attainable.)*

The formation of the group that in this case suggests the order of the *Assembly* has been a topic of much debate over the years since its first formations. The most crucial element discussed by Freud is to grasp the concept of why the group was originally formed rather than examining the emotional underlying religious beliefs and practices held common by the people of that 'pact' (Bocock, R., 1976 Pp. 77).

Freud asserts that the origin of religious attitude can be traced back to the feeling of infantile helplessness (Freud 1927 Pp. 72). He then attributes that an illusion is important for those that seek value in their lives as it gives them a sense of purpose (Freud 1927 Pp. 75). Although Freud did not give an explicit and technical definition of 'illusion' (Lear, J., 2005 Pp. 210), it is clear that Freud ascertained that they are, *'fulfilments of the oldest, strongest and most urgent wishes of mankind'* (Freud 1927 Pp. 30). However, the importance of this illusion is greatly misinterpreted due to the condition of humankind, as a great deal of guilt is attached to the development of civilization (Freud 1927 Pp. 61). This in turn, demonstrates that the formation of the religious group has its roots deeply embedded within an instinctual impulse, that of an acquired sense of guilt, stemming from the Oedipus complex (Freud 1927 Pp. 131) that has been repressed. Freud states that guilt is a consequence of an instinctual trend that undergoes repression. The libido processes are then turned into symptoms and its aggressive components into a sense of guilt (Freud 1927 Pp. 139).

A turning away from reality is required in order to sustain a sense of happiness. A re-assertion of habit and ideal is therefore rejuvenated towards an illusion of displaced contentment. The individual is therefore neurotic, *'he cannot tolerate the amount of frustration which society imposes on him in the service of its cultural ideals,'* (Freud 1927 Pp. 87), and turns to sanctuary in a form of a 'religious group', the reality is too formidable to bear.

The way in which order is asserted to construct a group of any that subscribe to an illusion is of great value to the formation of religious ideals. This is where the individual and the ideal 'illusion' marry up to form the *'unconditional submission'* (Freud 1927 Pp. 85) of the herd (Freud 1921 Pp. 81).

Order allows the individual to proceed accordingly within line of the group's expectation. Without order, group formation is formidable. The importance of order lies within its structure to maintain. For the *Assembly* to function the ideal 'illusion' must find a primal place within the groups order.

Freud suggests that civilization requires beauty, cleanliness and order for it to function and maintain (Freud 1927 Pp. 93). He then further suggests that order is a kind of compulsion to repeat. This is most evident within the *Assembly* as a predominant factor. Order is built within the cannons of the early Church, as exhibited in the New King James Bible (Romans chapter 12, 1 Corinthians chapter 12, and Ephesians chapter 4) and is exercised in a ritualistic way. The group sustain their convictions through the endurance of previous histories of punishment and martyrdom. In a very real sense this is how the individual measures the strength of his or her faith, through the up-holding of religious doctrine by sacrifice and denial of particular pleasures. This type of behaviour is adopted and employed by the followers based on their primary notion of exampled behaviour by other members of the following. Hence, the group by consensus will follow the illusion-ideal.

According to Le Bon what is of most particular interest within the group is the following (Freud 1921 Pp. 72). The strength of the group lies within the diluted acquirements of the individuals. In this way their distinctiveness vanishes (Freud 1921 Pp. 74) they become one mind carried away by a common impulse. McDougall (1920) calls this *'the principle of direct induction of emotion by way of the primitive sympathetic response'* (Freud 1921 Pp. 84). The individual enters the herd like a susceptible child. Freud quotes that the greater the numbers of people that observe a simultaneous affect, the stronger does this automatic compulsion grow (Freud 1921 Pp. 84). This in turn, signifies the common conception of an ideal that is presented to the group on the basis of an illusion. However, this illusion is woven and developed by suggestion of each and every individual not just by the leader (Freud 1921 Pp. 117-118).

The formation of the group and its order has so far been thus identified of requiring three major key elements; firstly, an illusion that permits its followers to invest their love within an ego-ideal. Secondly, an unconditional submission that expresses itself via a compulsion to repeat, and finally, the regulation of the illusion by suggestion of each individual, the 'common impulse'.

In order for the *Assembly* to self-sustain as an exclusive group it is vital that an influential factor is effective in insuring its order. In this case Freud identifies that an amount of guilt has to be invested within the group for the illusion to have achieved its effect, *'they claim to redeem mankind from this sense of guilt, which they call sin'* (Freud 1921 Pp. 136). Order, is then assured based on the principle aim of an unconscious urge for self gratification which is then repressed by the ego. This is a principle factor of Freud's theory of the libido, *'We distinguish this libido in respect of its special origin from the energy which must be supposed to underlie mental processes in general, and we thus also attribute a qualitative character to it'* (Freud 1905 Pp. 217).

The ensuring factor that keeps in suspension the whole process of re-generating the guilt experienced by the individual is an agency called the 'super-ego', first introduced by Freud in 1923 with his works on 'The Ego and the Id', *'the super-ego's role in relation to the ego may be compared to that of a judge or a censor'*, (Laplanche, J., and Pontalis, J.-B., 2006 Pp. 435).

Freud hypothesized that the sense of guilt is the most important problem in the development of civilisation and that the super-ego is the responsible agent that secures the individual's earliest object relations (Freud 1927 Pp. 61). It is assumed by Freud that it was as a consequence that the primal killing of the Father by the group of brothers should raise this great sense of guilt that springs from the Oedipus complex (Freud 1927 pp. 131).

A direct comparison can be made to the formation of the *Assembly* based upon the most crucial element of the super-ego's function of tormenting the sinful ego (Freud 1927 Pp. 125). The primal father has been executed; therefore, the love object of the group is now invested within an illusion of the ego-ideal. Social anxiety by the loss of love is the way in which the super-ego dominates the individual's intentions and keeps the group together.

Freud's term Eros which he refers to in the platonic sense, should be introduced here as the underlying drive that ensures the group's formation of unity. The fear of this loss of love is enough to cultivate the illusion. The process that governs order under the restraint of the illusion is very mechanical in nature. It is dependent on the *'libidinal ties'* that characterize the group (Freud 1921 Pp. 101). Order now demonstrates itself within the framework of an active agent, namely, the libido, *'which attaches itself to the satisfaction of the great vital needs, and chooses as its first objects the people who have a share in that process'* (Freud 1921 Pp. 103).

The group formation of the *Assembly* is an equivalent to the social bond that takes place as a consequence of the execution of the primal father. It shares its qualities on the notion of an impulse that dominates the individual's intentions and solidifies the ideal concept of the illusion. The illusion is the intention of the individual and the individual invests in the common belief of the group. However, the structure of the group remains the centre of the illusion, and it is in that that the individual invests his or her concept of the ideal. Without the group the illusion ideal lays dormant.

Bibliography

Bocock, R. (1976) Freud and Modern Society: An outline and analysis of Freud's sociology, Thomas Nelson and Sons Ltd, Great Britain.

Freud, S. (1905), 'Three essays on sexuality'. The Standard Edition of the Complete Psychological Works, Strachey, J. ed., in collaboration with Anna Freud., Re-printed 2001, Volume 7, Vintage Publishers, Great Britain.

Freud, S. (1921) 'Group Psychology', The Standard Edition of the Complete Psychological Works of Sigmund Freud, Strachey, J. ed., in collaboration with Anna Freud., Re-printed in 2001, Volume 18, Vintage publications, Great Britain.

Freud, S. (1923), 'The Ego and the Id'. The Standard Edition of the Complete Psychological Works, Strachey, J. ed., in collaboration with Anna Freud., Re-printed 2001, Volume 19, Vintage Publishers, Great Britain.

Freud, S. (1927) 'Civilization and its Discontents'. The Standard Edition of the Complete Psychological Works, Strachey, J. ed., in collaboration with Anna Freud., Re-printed in 2001, Volume 21, Vintage publications, Great Britain.

Laplanche, J., and Pontalis, J.-B. (2006) The Language of Psychoanalysis, Karnac books, London.

Lear, J. (2005) 'Freud - Morality and Religion', re-printed 2006 Routledge Publishers, New York, USA.

Nelson, T. (1992) The New King James Bible, 'Book of: Romans, Corinthians & Ephesians', 1992, Inc. Republic of Korea.

The Case of Dora:

Dora's first dream, her feelings towards her mother re-examined and Freud's failure to interpret the transference.

The case concerning Dora has been the topic of much discussion and debate over the past century. The elements it consists of make it one of the most interesting and complicated cases that Freud ever engaged in and highlights some of his weaknesses and strengths regarding the practice of Psychoanalysis. A critical point to mention is that this case is as much about Freud as it is about Dora, in that although Freud's mechanical methodology is one that employs a scientific approach to behavioural interpretation, he asserts his laws of what he believes to be correct to this case only to discover that his approach is questionable due to the result (or lack of result). As it shall be demonstrated it is clear that a problem of transference is in question and not, so to speak, his line of practice or the interpretation of Dora's first dream; although this paper attempts to re-examine Dora's relationship with her mother and re-assert her in a new light.

The story runs like a poetic genre, what may seem as a problematic case for Freud is a beautiful love story for the reader that leaves one with an open mind to shed light on the dynamics of Psychoanalysis and the problems it faces. This case was crucial in order for Freud to develop his practice further as it addresses transference and counter-transference as two components, that at the time Freud himself was only getting acquainted with (Steven Marcus 1985 Pp. 89).

Dora's case began in autumn 1900. Dora was a young lady of eighteen years, she was very reluctant at first to engage with Freud in analysis. As a critique from face value it would seem that Dora had developed a very strong willed personality that had carried her through her teenage years, one might suspect that this is due to the unsavoury events that she experienced with her close friends as they are identified as Herr K. and Frau K. (husband and wife, friends of the family). Hence, this could allude to suggest that Dora had no problem in expressing her reluctance to undergo therapy, whereas a young girl may have felt embarrassed to express her reluctance for analysis especially as this could be contrived by a professional and elder such as Freud as ill mannered behaviour; Dora finds no shame in what she exhibits in terms of her behaviour. However, what must not be overlooked is that Freud had already been acquainted with the family before Dora's analysis commenced. This has an important implication of familiarity and poses a problem during analysis. An important point to highlight is that Freud notices and states that *'Dora, had even at the age of eight begun to develop neurotic symptoms'* (Freud 1905 Pp. 21).

It should be noted that Dora was a very misfortunate individual as she suffered with various symptoms such as dyspnoea, a nervous cough (which would sometimes result in a loss of voice), and migraines. In fact, Dora had been presented to Freud by her father two years prior when she was sixteen with complaints of a cough and hoarseness, Freud offered treatment but her ill condition had diminished before any treatment had been administered. Before Dora engaged in therapy it is made evident that she had been under a tremendous amount of mental strain and confusion that looked likely to have stemmed from a question of sexual identity. Freud is able to locate a great deal of Dora's fantasies and wish-fulfilments through analysing a dream reported by her. The dream is a rich source of how to understand Dora's personal intentions and how she really feels about her family as well as herself. However, throughout the whole case lies a theme of sexual motive and identity which, in turn, leads to a case of hysteria.

Within this case there is much emphasis placed on Herr K. as Freud emphasises his motives and his attempts of possessing Dora in a sexual way. This is demonstrated by Herr K. in his place of business as he *'clasped the girl to him and pressed a kiss upon her lips'* (Freud 1905 Pp. 28). Herr K. is very much an influential figure within Freud's interpretation of Dora's dream and attributes much of her underlying desire towards him. However, the case is not so straight forward as it yields a question of unconscious desire that pertains to others, as shall be demonstrated.

According to Freud's work on the *'Interpretation of dreams'* published in 1900, he asserts that dreams are wish-fulfilments, satisfying in the unconscious dream state what can not be satisfied in reality. Dora's first dream begins *'A house was on fire. My father was standing beside my bed and woke me up. I dressed quickly. Mother wanted to stop and save her jewel-case; but Father said: "I refuse to let myself and my two children be burnt for the sake of your jewel-case." We hurried downstairs, and as soon as I was outside I woke up.'* (Freud 1905 Pp. 64).

Freud believes that the dream demonstrates Dora's fears of this man 'Herr K.' forcing his way into her room, therefore her jewel case is in danger and if anything happens to it her father will be at fault. Hence, Dora chose a situation of the opposite, that her father should save her from harms way (Freud 1905 Pp. 69). Freud then continues to suggest that everything in the dream is turned into its opposite, in this respect the mother is a clear example of what Freud is alluding to, *'In the incident of the bracelet, you would have been glad to accept what your mother had rejected. Now let us put "give" instead of "accept" and "withhold" instead of "reject". Then it means that you were ready to give your father what your mother withheld from him; and the thing in question was connected with jewellery.'* (Freud 1905 Pp. 70). Freud's interpretation of this dream specimen evokes the assumption that Dora is embodied within her mother's behaviour. When Freud questions Dora about the jewel-case she confesses that Herr K. presented her with an expensive jewel-case a little time before (Freud 1905 Pp. 69). Freud places a great deal of emphasis on the jewel-case and suggests that *'a return-present would have been very appropriate'* (Freud 1905 Pp. 69). Freud then reiterates this notion again, *'He gave you a jewel-case; so you are to give him your jewel-case'* (Freud 1905 Pp. 70). However, what is interesting here is that Freud shifts the return gift from being an object gift as first mentioned onto being *'her'* jewel-case. "Jewel-case" [Schmuckkastchen] can also serve as an expression for the female genitals (Freud 1905 Pp. 69). If this is correct this should demonstrate the wish-fulfilment component of the dream. Although a great deal of displacement is exhibited the true sense of Dora's feelings are, as Freud points out, embedded within her love for Herr K *'in short, these efforts prove once more how deeply you loved him'* (Freud 1905 Pp. 70).

Freud suggests that the dream sets up a connection between Dora's childhood experience and the present day with the intention of re-shaping the present day on the model of the past (Freud 1905 Pp. 71). Freud's connection here stems from Dora's bed wetting as Dora herself clarifies that *"an accident might happen at night"* and that *"it might be necessary to leave the room"* (Freud 1905 Pp. 72). In Freud's later work's of 'an infantile neurosis' he makes an assumption that the reaction of shame is connected with the emptying of the bladder (Freud 1919 Pp. 92n). It may be that Dora harboured some sort of shame that expressed itself within the dream, perhaps shame towards her mother for not having in possession her 'jewel-case' and needing to collect it. Freud then goes on to say that Dora experienced bed wetting up to a later age than is expected. Achieving this result clearly demonstrates the nature of the therapy Freud was employing, a regressive technique. Regression in its most simplistic form is a reverting to a primitive or childlike pattern of behaviour (Reber, A 1995 Pp. 649). With Freud's regressive technique highlighted this case in retrospect can be further examined to clarify an important implication to do with Dora's mother in the dream.

Dora's mother attempts to save her jewel case. However, Dora is not sure how her mother got into the dream, she was not with her at L_____ at the time (Freud 1905 Pp. 69). Perhaps Dora's mother in the dream acts as a type of protector and saviour for Dora. If the dream is to demonstrate a wish-fulfilment then perhaps it is within Dora's mother that this is fulfilled in conjunction with the jewel-case.

There is a rich source of information in the dream that pertains to how Dora feels about her parents from this dream. After considering the time, place, and Dora's report of how she felt the dream serves only to confirm that there is a deeper involvement between Dora and her mother, *'The relations between the girl and her mother had been unfriendly for years,'* (Freud 1905 Pp. 20). The dream could be an attempt for an unconscious reconciliation between Dora and her mother, a struggle to place her mother where any young girl would want her to be in cases such as an emergency, as a protector over her. However, from what is known about Dora's relationship with her mother it is strange that Dora should place such faith within her, once more being a woman that she speaks ill of. Within the dream there is a desperate attempt made to salvage what Dora prides most 'the jewel-case', however, a most interesting and overlooked connection is exhibited, Dora's value for the jewel-case is infused with her mother, it can be further interpreted that her mother is in fact a representation of this jewel-case, her female genitals, an object down trodden by those that Dora so desperately seeks acceptance. Furthermore there is a resemblance between the jewel-case and Dora's mother, the fact that they are both the object of relentless pain. In short Dora's mother had been rejected by her father to some degree in that he holds something against her, *'you know already that I get nothing out of my own wife'* (Freud 1905 Pp. 26). If this is the case then there is an added dimension to the interpretation of Dora's dream namely the concern of her mother's presence and the object of pain that both parties share. Dora and her mother in sum are as equals to the man that rejects them. It is entirely possible that although Dora was on very bad terms with her mother (Freud 1905 Pp. 23) she would have also developed feelings of sympathy towards her too as *'her mother was suffering from abdominal pains and from a discharge (a catarrh)...It was Dora's view – and here again she was probably right – that this illness was due to her father, who had thus handed on his venereal disease to her mother'*, (Freud 1905 Pp. 75). Also, with reports of being a witness of her father's affair to Frau K. this all contributes to assert that Dora may have reserved a sympathetic side towards her mother harboured with emotion. According to Lewin (1973) Freud failed to recognise this and what she really wanted was *'the total, exclusive and absolute love of her mother'* (Gregorio Kohon 1986 Pp. 367).

However, equally weighted with importance and should not be dismissed is the question of displacement that is apparent within the dream. This can be understood as to what is already known of Dora's relationship and closeness with Frau K. Dora's mother in the dream could be a representation of three people, Dora, Dora's mother and Frau K. all of which are women. The reason Dora should be represented within this dream as her mother is that the jewel-case has a sentimental value that only the dreamer could know of, illustrated as thus, *'Mother wanted to stop and save her jewel-case'* (Freud 1905 Pp. 64). This statement is greatly important in determining what Dora places her life on. Dora demonstrates what the jewel-case (her genitals) mean to her as she would rather stay and collect it risking her own life then run outside immediately.

The connection here with Frau K. is only made evident by Freud's observation and interpretation of how Dora perceives Frau K. in light of her father's affair. An undercurrent of sexual impulses could explain this of the way Dora feels about this woman.

The house on fire could stand as a symbolic form of Dora's body under threat by Herr K. Freud asserts Fire as a phallic symbol (Freud 1931 Pp. 90) and like the nature of fire he enforces himself onto Dora, *'suddenly clasped the girl to him and pressed a kiss upon her lips'* (Freud 1905 Pp. 28). Dora's reaction to this is very similar to how she reacts in the dream *'tore herself free from the man, and hurried past him to the staircase and from there to the street door'* (Freud 1905 Pp. 28). Within the dream a staircase and running outside are both reported (Freud 1905 Pp. 64).

Her father's behaviour in the dream, on the other hand, demonstrates what is confirmed in reality, a lack of concern about Dora's jewel-case. Notice that the jewel-case belongs to Dora. A question of displacement arises. On one hand Dora reports her mother's concern for the jewel-case, however, the nature of a dream is always subjective to the dreamer and therefore any concern for an object within the dream would naturally come from the dreamer.

A problem of transference lies at the root of this failed case. Transference is an important process played by the analyzan that has its value in the actualisation of unconscious wishes. It is expected that the analyzan establishes a relationship with an object that evokes an unconscious response linking material to that object of infantile value, hence, *'in the transference, infantile prototypes re-emerge and are experienced with a strong sensation of immediacy'* (Laplanche, J., and Pontalis, J., 2006 Pp. 455).

According to Muslin and Gill (1978) Freud's mistake was in failing to interpret the transference enough (Kohon, G., 1986 Pp. 367). There are some possible explanations as to why. Some light can be shed on this problem by briefly examining Dora's later life. Over twenty years on from when Dora left Freud's treatment she was referred by her doctor to Felix Deutsch for consultation. Dora at this point had many symptoms that led her to ill health such as dizziness, loss of hearing (but not completely), insomnia, constipation, and chronic premenstrual pains. She also reports behavioural as well as psychological problems that have stemmed from traumatic events that she had experienced such as the death of her husband and her son leaving her, this in turn led to Dora's fears of sexual relations, her disgust in men and her rejection of a second pregnancy due to labour fears. The sad truth is that Dora expressed herself in a very desperate way, as described by Deutsch this led to an uncomfortable pressure for the people around her life to constantly hear complaints of anxiety attacks and chronic fear of death, *'her death from cancer of the colon was an acknowledged blessing for all those who surrounded her'* (Kohon, G., 1986 Pp. 369). With this report Deutsch (1957) then refers to her as one of the most *'repulsive hysterics'* he had met (Kohon, G., 1986 Pp. 369). Deutsch's report parallel's how Freud describes his difficulties working with Dora. He reports that she addressed new questions that related to problems of transference and homosexuality. This account of Dora by Deutsch is no less a contribution in understanding Freud's difficulties and problems he may have faced in dealing with Dora. However, Freud remains with the same mind in suggesting the problem of genital heterosexuality and the Oedipus complex was in question (Kohon, G., 1986 Pp. 369).

The most important aspect that Deutsch notes is when Dora exhibits flirtatious and seductive behaviour towards him when he discovers that Dora was actually a historic case of Freud's. Could this suggest that Freud was attracted and led on to be seduced by Dora? If this is the case it would lead to the problem of transference. Lacan (1951) asserts a similar assumption as he suggests that Freud had placed himself in the place of Herr K. The sexual identity of Dora poses a mighty struggle between Freud's first notion on the Oedipal theory and Dora's homosexuality, which becomes more apparent (Kohon, G., 1986 Pp. 369).

The sexual underlying theme of homosexuality is of great interest in unravelling this case and the deeper the analysis goes the more evident it is that a conflict of sexual impulses leads to the presence of a neurotic conflict.

This feature of homosexuality becomes more evident throughout the case and is a centre point that rests the explanation of Dora's intentions and behavioural disturbances, but how is this identified and how does Freud address it? Dora had obviously grown a passion of fondness towards Frau K. Freud notes that this fondness or love is exhibited by the way Dora had harboured and repressed feelings towards Frau K., *'the jealous emotions of a woman were linked in the unconscious with a jealousy such as might have been felt by a man'* (Freud 1905 Pp. 63). This statement could have explained the very notion behind Dora's fragile state of mind. Dora's self worth would have been affected on two accounts. This stems from the relationship that Frau K. built with Dora, a pretentious one, with the intention to gain closeness to her father and in the end betray her trust by disclosing personal information about Dora to Herr K. Also, *'the fact that she had been sacrificed by her father'* (Freud 1905 Pp. 62).

According to Freud there is a triangular affair taking place between Herr K, Frau K and Dora. Freud concludes the last chapter of 'the clinical picture' (standard edition, volume seven) demonstrating that Dora's speculation of the preceding events concerning her father had led her to suppress her love for Herr K. which had been conscious, however, she conceals her love for Frau K., which is in a deeper sense unconscious (Freud 1905 Pp. 62). However, this interpretation could be as a result of a developing counter-transference. An attempt is made by Freud to fit this case in line with his pre-existing notion on his Oedipal theory. This problem has been vindicated by Eric Erikson (1964) as he identified a problem that had sufficed in respect of Freud's counter-transference with both his own and Dora's adolescence; also insensitive to her adolescent conflict over wishing to be both independent and dependent. To sum up Erikson's opinion Freud was too insensitive towards this case (Mahony. P., 1932 Pp. 39). It could be at this point where Dora finds her most discomfort with Freud and expresses her difficulty. Here the analyzan struggles with her unconscious desire concerning a homosexual matter.

After revising this case it seems to be the most probable explanation that Freud, to reiterate Lacan (1951), is led away in his intervention and concerns himself in the nature of his belief in an ideal. The result: a natural Oedipus complex arises, *'his need* (Freud) *to insist upon Dora's love for Herr K. as a displacement of her love for her father'* (Kohon, G., 1986 Pp. 369). According to Krohn and Krohn (1972) they identify that this may have been the case, however, address that the underlying suppression actually stemmed from her phallic attachment to her mother (Kohon, G., Pp. 379). This concludes to suggest that although an unconscious identification was formed with her father, it served to act as *'a defence against her hostility and rivalry with him or as an expression of an unconscious wish to love woman as a man'* (Kohon, G., 1986 Pp. 379). It is evident that Dora was a victim of a therapy which did not comprehend her underlying impulse of a sexual nature towards another woman. The dream confirms Dora's fragile state of mind that exposes her vulnerability and could further testify a low self of worth she has towards her most precious possession 'the jewel-case' [Schmuckkastchen].

Bibliography

Bernhiemer, C., and Kahane, C., Editors., In Dora's Case, Freud-Hysteria-Feminism, (1990) Second Edition, Columbia University Press, New York:
    Chapter 3: Marcus, S., Freud and Dora: Story, History, Case History.

Freud, S. (1901-1905), 'A Case of Hysteria'. The Standard Edition of the Complete Psychological Works, Re-printed 2001, Volume 7, Vintage Publishers, Great Britain.

Freud, S. (1917-1919), 'An Infantile Neurosis and Other Works'. The Standard Edition of the Complete Psychological Works, Re-printed 2001, Volume 17, Vintage Publishers, Great Britain.

Freud, S. (1927-1931), 'Civilization and its Discontents'. The Standard Edition of the Complete Psychological Works, Re-printed 2001, Volume 21, Vintage Publishers, Great Britain.

Kohon, G., The British School of Psychoanalysis, The Independent Tradition, (1986), Free Association Books, Great Britain, London.

Laplanche, J., and Pontalis, J.-B., The Language of Psychoanalysis, (2006) Karnac books, Great Britain.

Mahony, P., Freud's Dora, A Psychoanalytic, Historical, and Textual Staudy, 1932 (1996), Yale University Press, New Haven and London.

The Wolf-Man:
Belief in God the Father as the Wolf

The Wolf-Man case is probably one of the most technical cases that Freud ever engaged in. It effectively demonstrates Freud's psychoanalytical skills with his ability to interpret a vivid dream, as well as apply the right psychoanalytical method.

The Wolf-Man was born on Christmas Eve 1886, according to the Julian calendar (6 January 1887 according to the Gregorian calendar), on his father's estate on the banks of Dnieper, north of the provincial city Kherson. He lived with his mother and father during his childhood and had a sister two years older than him. As his family were very wealthy it was common that his parents would spend long periods of time away from the estate engaged with either business or pleasure and the Wolf-Man would be looked after by his Nanya and the Governess that changed every so often.

The Wolf-Man had a very difficult emotional up-bringing. He had a phobia of wolves that dominated much of his early years, which was partly fuelled by his older sister who tormented him (Freud 1918 Pp. 16) by making sexual advances on him (Freud 1918 Pp. 20) whether intentionally or unintentionally, that later had an effect on the Wolf-Man's sexual identity. However, it was clear that the Wolf-Man had an infantile neurosis that had been identified and elaborated on by Freud. Freud divided the Wolf-Mans childhood into two phases: the first phase of naughtiness and perversity from his seduction just over three years old up to his fourth birthday, and a longer phase in which signs of his neurosis predominated (Freud 1918 Pp. 28).

Freud identified the division of the boy's two phases by a dream that he had, in which, the boy awoke from being in a state of panic and anxiety; *'I dreamt that it was night and that I was lying in my bed. (My bed stood with its foot towards the window; in front of the window there was a row of old walnut trees. I know it was winter when I had the dream, and night-time.) Suddenly the window opened of its own accord, and I was terrified to see that some white wolves were sitting on the big walnut tree in front of the window. There were six or seven of them. The wolves were quite white, and looked more like foxes or sheep-dogs, for they had big tails like foxes and they had their ears pricked like dogs when they pay attention to something. In great terror, evidently of being eaten up by the wolves, I screamed and woke up,'* (Freud 1918 Pp. 29).

What is interesting about this dream is that all the attention is directed toward the child, there is a very real sense of fear such as; it being night, the bed stood, window opening of its own accord and six or seven wolves looking at him. However, the most chilling report of the dream is that the wolves *'had their ears pricked like dogs when they pay attention to something'*, as this emphasises the anxiety that the child must have felt. It is within this suspended picture of terror that the unknowing demonstrates a great fear towards the child. The child's fear develops as his thoughts are directed to what 'he thinks the wolves know and what they know he knows'. An undercurrent of intelligent dialogue is being constructed within the dream between the wolves and the child; the child demonstrates that he is an enemy to himself, as all the characters of the dream are naturally constructed by the dreamer. It is not as clear who or what is the dominant factor within the dream, however, it is possible that the boy is the least dominant. An unconscious wish-fulfilment can be exhibited in relation to this dominance and further more self-torture.

The child's conscious recollection of the six or seven wolves (the number of a possible threat), alludes to an existing unconscious concept of fear associated with this number. It is unlikely the child would have counted the wolves in the dream. In this case the wolves and the number of them must have pre-existed in his mind and he must have been unconsciously aware of this.

The open window could represent an 'emotional barrier of fear' that has been removed. The fear does not start with the wolves themselves but the positioning of the wolves on the tree. Effort is exerted with the window opening and the bed standing on its leg in order to achieve the goal, and the child is aware of this. However, he is focused on the fear of suspense and not the dynamics and implications of the dream. This dream yields a religious component that the boy, and to some extent Freud, may have overlooked.

The bed yields a sexual implication in that it represents private space. The bed is where the infant can be active in ways where no one can observe, a type of freedom is associated with the bed. However, the dream restricts the child of this luxury. This could be as a result of the boy's acquaintance with religion. The religious stories of God being everywhere could be a result of feeling self-conscious and therefore, having a dream where even in the most private of places the child is intensely observed. This in turn leads to paranoia, as the power lies within the stillness of the scene an amplified uncomfortable scenario of self awareness is felt. The child wakes up in a panic screaming, with a feeling of anxiety, *'I think this was my first anxiety-dream'*, (Freud 1918 Pp. 29).

The infant has felt a restriction within the dream and a conflict is formed. It is at this point that the child feels anxiety. It is also at this point that an infantile neurosis can be identified, *'Anxiety is a problem rather of neurosis, and all that remains to be discussed is how it comes about that anxiety can arise under dream conditions'*, (Freud 1925 Pp. 135).

Freud noted that the child developed *'a severe neurotic disturbance, which began immediately before his fourth birthday, as an anxiety-hysteria (in the shape of an animal phobia), then changed into an obsessional neurosis with a religious content, and lasted with its offshoots as far as into his tenth year'*, (Freud 1918 Pp. 8). According to Freud's work on 'the future of an illusion' (1927), he stated that for a child to successfully complete his or her development to the civilised stage, he or she must first pass through a phase of neurosis. This is due to the instinctual demands that the child can not suppress by rational operation but are repressed, behind which lies the motive of anxiety (Freud 1927 Pp. 42-43). Freud then leads on to theorise that, *'religion would thus be the universal obsessional neurosis of humanity'... 'It arose out of the Oedipus complex, out of the relation to the father'* (Freud 1927 Pp. 43).

Although an uncomfortable feeling is felt by the child during this dream it is evident that there is still a wish-fulfilment attached to the dream. Whilst the child is confronted with the wolves they acknowledge the child and remain suspended, there is no mention of them actively moving toward the child in a threatening way. The dream exhibits these wolves under submission.

The child's behaviour of how he responds after the dream parallels how he acts towards a picture that his sister presents him with, the purpose, to torment him (Freud 1918 Pp. 16). As a young child the Wolf-Man had been tormented by his older sister showing him a particular picture of a wolf standing upright. This always made him scream and say, "The wolf is coming to eat me up" (Freud

1918 Pp. 16). However, it is within this picture that the unusual characteristic of the wolf standing upright might be connected with the unusual positioning of the wolves in the tree within the dream. The same feeling may have been felt by the boy, this feeling of unease that these animals (the wolves) should find themselves positioned in an unnatural way, all centred towards him. This could lead to the boy equating the wolves with mystical powers in a supernatural sense; like a man who can fly, or a rabbit that can talk. A direct link can be made between the wolves and the boy's religion. In both cases, that of the dream and that of the picture, there is no real threat of danger, however, there is clearly a visual emotional negative effect. It seems that the picture alone of the wolf is enough to create an emotional damaging response that results with the infant screaming. The child must have associated a fear of the wolf with the motive of his sister. This could further suggest that the boy had been traumatized and the effects of this are reflected in the dream.

The dream organises the whole of the neurosis, whilst the unconscious interprets elements of the dream. The signifiers selected to construct a neurosis are predominantly the imaginary experience with wolves. As the unconscious is unlimited the material then is flexible so the child's dream can be an intensifying experience of anxiety.

The dream has mystical significance as well as unconscious influences that contribute to neurotic behaviour. For example, unconscious recollection of fear vulnerability pertains to the wolves' existence within the dream. The story of 'The Wolf and the Seven Little Goats' (Freud 1918 Pp. 30) that his Grandfather used to tell includes the death of the wolf that contributes to a self-conscious death instinct.

All the material demonstrates an infantile neurosis. It can be observed that there are two sections to this, that of anxiety and that of obsessional neurosis. This is an advanced dream for a child of nearly four years of age (Freud 1918 Pp. 8).

A significant factor of the dream could be by implication the relationship between the Wolf-Man and his father. This can be demonstrated through the concept of displacement. It is clear that the wolves represent a fear of some kind, perhaps attributed to an authority within the child's life. The relationship between the child and his father had uncomfortably intensified, *'fear of his father became the dominating factor'* (Freud 1918 Pp. 17). The significance of how this affects the Wolf-Man is verified when it is considered that his father is his admirable model. His intention was to become: *'a gentlemen like his father'* (Freud 1918 Pp. 27).

Freud describes that the metamorphism of child development in religious belief is a procedure that is tailored by the relationship exhibited between the child and the father. From the time the child is born he develops libido and then follows the paths of narcissistic needs. In this way the mother is said to be the child's first love-object as she satisfies the child's hungers and protects the child against dangers that threaten him in the external world. The protection that the mother offers is soon replaced by the father throughout the rest of childhood. However, there is a conflicting attitude associated with the child's perception of the father, as the father himself constitutes a threat to the child. Freud believes that this could be due to the father's earlier relation to the child's mother. To put it bluntly, there is a love-hate relationship towards the father. The child fears him no less then he longs for him and admires him (Freud 1927 Pp. 24). It is at this point that Freud asserts that *'the indications of this ambivalence in the attitude to the father are deeply imprinted in every religion'* (Freud 1927 Pp. 24). It can be suggested that the Wolf-Man invested his love within an object relating to his beliefs in God the Father. There is a similarity between the child's perception of the wolf and his father. It is only through the Wolf-Man's account of how he embraces his religion and reacts to religious doctrine that a similarity can be made. So in order to fully appreciate this case attention should be placed upon the Wolf-Man's religious up-bringing.

As a child the Wolf-Man was first introduced to religion by his mother. His questioning of Christianity was first sparked by a picture he saw of the Czech Reformer Huss being burned at the stake. His mother explained to him who Christ was and the significance of the crucifixion and as he was growing up his Nanya would sometimes tell him stories about the saints and martyrs (Gardiner, M., 1989 Pp. 9). This intrigued him and he developed a religious Christian faith, *'I gradually became very religious myself and began to concern myself with the Christian doctrine'*, (Gardiner, M., 1989 Pp. 9). This evidence of the Wolf-Man's account of Christianity demonstrates that he was probably subjected to traumatising stories of people who shared the same faith in Christianity and were punished for it.

The Wolf-Man's religious enquiry leads him to ask a question that has a profound implication pertaining to the dream. This is of his knowledge of God being omnipotent. Within the dream the child feels invaded of his private space. This could be as a result of his conscious questioning and battling with the concept of God. However, it is with the crucifixion of Jesus Christ that the boy doubted his faith toward God, *'I began to doubt why, if God was so all-powerful, the crucifixion of His Son was necessary'*, (Gardiner, M., 1989 Pp. 9). As a result of this doubt he was led to feel tormented and like he had sinned. The dream confirms this in two main key areas. Firstly, by the unconscious fear of the unknown re-interpreted in the figure of the wolves, that serve as a symbolic figure of the authority of God and his father, and secondly his power of submission over his fear; over the wolves.

In order to re-interpret this dream the emphasis should focus on the relationship between the Wolf-Man's religion and mental state. The dream itself can be understood through preceding events that influenced the image congregated of the wolves and could also explain the scenario of being in bed looking out of the open window. However, the question of significance within the dream lies with the emotional response that the child exhibits during the suspended period of the wolves in the tree looking at him.

One conclusion that can be drawn from the child's emotional response can be that the child wished for the wolves to devour him. As this did not occur the child responded in a type of panic. There may have been an expectancy for the wolves to have 'punished' the boy. Freud confirms that the boy developed a desired masochistic sexual satisfaction as he would try to force *'punishments'* and *'beatings'* out of his father (Freud 1918 Pp. 28). Freud later comments that, *'his screaming fits were therefore simply attempts at seduction'* (Freud 1918 Pp. 28). An explanation for this, according to Freud, could be of the great amount of guilt that the child harboured (Freud 1918 Pp. 28). This could be in relation to his identity and religious piety. The sexual implication of identity is in question, as it is suggested that an identified characteristic of the boy's neurosis was his *'primary feminine impulses'* (Freud 1918 Pp. 6). This is a dominating factor throughout the case that is influenced by his religious conviction as to the relationship with his father, a representation of 'God the Father' now manifested as the 'Wolf'.

An outstanding feature of the Wolf-Man was his susceptibility to religious stories and how literally he considered what he was told from the people he respected and loved. An example of his susceptibility is evident when his Nanya threatens him for masturbating in front of her, *'children who do that, she added, got a 'wound' in the place'*, (Freud 1918 Pp. 24). Quite naturally this fixed a fear that the boy became a bondservant to that restricted him from masturbating. Freud notes that due to the suppression of masturbation, the child's sexual life was compromised and instead of naturally heading toward the genital zone he *'gave way before an external obstacle, and was thrown back by its influence into an earlier phase of pregenital organisation'* (Freud 1918 Pp. 25), also as a consequence *'the boy's sexual life took on a sadistic-anal character'* (Freud 1918 Pp. 26). This demonstrates that the boy was vulnerable to religious misconceptions due to his susceptibility. The boy interprets his religious doctrinal teachings that he had been brought up on as an imaginary fear of castration, a fear of loss, a fear that is very real and that is invested in his intentions. With the knowledge of an omnipresent God, the boy is now aware that he is being watched and judged even within his most private of places.

The child experiences great anxiety within the dream as he witnesses the wolves on the tree watching him. This could hypothetically demonstrate a paternal threat made in response to his sexual activities. His father, displaced in the dream as the wolves are condensed as the representation of 'God the Father'. The wolf in this case is imbued by the child as his threat of castration, *'the result for him is an intense castration anxiety'*, (Laplanche, J., & Pontalis, J.,-B.).

Freud elaborates on why the wolf should be selected to represent the boy's fear of castration. He notes that the boy reported a story that he had heard told by his grandfather of a wolf who had leapt into a tailors room by an open window. The tailor catches the wolf and pulls off it's tail, (Freud 1918 Pp. 31).

The religious implication of the dream expands the intensity of the boy's anxiety. It contributes to the boy's feeling of paranoia and confirms that there is a sense of guilt played by the boy. It is as a result of the Wolf-Man's religious faith that foundation of an illusionary complexity is built, for example the suspended motion between the wolves and the boy exhibits a 'theory of mind' concept. The boy has the ability to be self-aware and is of the knowledge that others also have awareness (Cartwright, J., 2000 Pp. 355). In this capacity the boy is thinking what he thinks the wolves are thinking.

This case demonstrates the complex strategy involved in investigating the root cause and the formation of an infantile neurosis. Freud considered three main areas of concern; the boy's relationship to his fears of the wolf through his religious exposition, his relationship to his father, and the restriction of masturbation due to fear formation. These are the most predominant indicators that contribute to the formation of the Wolf-Man's neurosis. What is clear is that this case can never be exhausted. There are many implications as to why the Wolf-Man suffered so much as a child and to what extent the Wolf-Man interpreted the dream to signify his wish-fulfilment as well as his fears. There is certainly a religious influence within the dream and arguably the child's earlier life. Although there are difficulties in dissecting this case such as the required great deal of regression, Freud nevertheless, demonstrated his ability to interpret a dream and discover an infantile neurosis.

Bibliography

Cartwright, J. (2000) Evolution and Human Behaviour, Darwinian Perspectives on Human Nature, Palgrave.

Freud, S. (1917-1919), 'An Infantile Neurosis and Other Works'. The Standard Edition of the Complete Psychological Works, Strachey, J. ed., in collaboration with Anna Freud, Re-printed 2001, Volume 17, Vintage Publishers, Great Britain.

Freud, S. (1927) 'The Future of an Illusion'. The Standard Edition of the Complete Psychological Works, Strachey, J. ed., in collaboration with Anna Freud, Volume twenty-one, Vintage Publications, Great Britain.

Freud, S. (1923-1925) 'The Ego and the Id and Other Works'. The Standard Edition of the Complete Psychological Works, Strachey, J. ed., in collaboration with Anna Freud, Re-printed 2001, Volume 19, Vintage Publishers, Great Britain.

Gardiner, M. (1972) the Wolf-Man and Sigmund Freud, The Institute of Psycho-analysis, Karnac Books.

Laplanche, J., and Pontalis, J.-B., (2006) The Language of Psychoanalysis, Re-printed 1989, Karnac books, Great Britain.

A Mind-Body Connection:

A developing theory of therapy for people that suffer with Wernicke's Aphasia (Damage to the left side of the brain that processes language)

This paper considers the possible implications of a proposed theory that suggests a picture drawing method for patients in therapy that suffer with Wernicke's aphasia as a complimentary technique to assist in free association. In this way, this new method should provide substitutive information about the patient where due to their condition of Wernicke's aphasia free association might be a problematic technique. As the free association method is meant to extract information direct from the unconscious the relationship between unconscious processing and the theoretical implications of conscious functioning whilst engaged in free association will be examined.

A developing hypothesis that can propose a theory of therapy for those that suffer with Wernicke's aphasia, would contribute to the existing information that there is on this subject as well as complement the psychoanalytic tradition of therapy that relies so much on language and its functions. This investigation considers and interweaves the psychoanalytical theory of mind with pre-existing evidence in neuroscience.

In order to fully appreciate psychological explanations of human behaviour it is important to include a theory of function that operates on the most rudimentary level. In which case, to understand the mind one must examine the biological processes of the brain and nervous system in order to identify a systemic mode of behaviour that can be traced to biological functions.

To demonstrate how effective Psychoanalytic therapy could be by employing a picture drawing method for patients with Wernicke's aphasia it is essential to consider Marian Annett's right shift theory. Annett (1985) imbues an interesting theory of the genotype playing an important role in hand dominance as well as hemisphere dominance (Annett, M. 1985 Pp. 291-292). The procedure would be first to clarify the patient's handedness in measure of visuo-spatial ability. According to Annett's hypothesis this should yield as a positive correlation in order to certify hemispheric function. Therefore, methods of interpretation should be developed to gain a clearer insight to the patient's mental functioning. This is the equivalent to the psychoanalytic free association method which was developed by Sigmund Freud (Freud 1893 Pp. 56). This allows a patient with a language deficiency to express his or her feelings and thoughts via a process that does not require the full attention of the Wernicke's area that processes the formation language.

It is important to highlight that within therapy the patient and psychoanalyst form a bond that incorporates a play theory. It is based on this assumption that the psychoanalytic session should take the dynamics of 'playing' where the patient can be creative and with this feel free (Winnicott, D. 1971 Pp. 71). Therefore, play needs to be the underlying theme that structures the session. Melanie Klein emphasis 'Play technique' as equivalent to the process of free association. With this notion in place it can be suggested that free association is not just limited by one method but can extend to many different methods so long as play remains the essential feature.

Free association

A key cornerstone in psychoanalytic technique is embedded within the use of free association, *'method according to which voice must be given to all thoughts without exception which enter the mind, whether such thoughts are based upon a specific element (word, number, dream-image or any kind of idea at all) or produced spontaneously'* (Laplanche, J. & Pontalis, J.-B. 2006 Pp. 169).

Free association was first stumbled across by Josef Breuer's patient (Anna O.) in 1881. Breuer devised a technique with his patient in which he would hear her out, and by doing so, would follow her lead and build a set of appropriate structures for understanding her talk. By collaborating with Freud, both Breuer and Freud came to certain conclusions as to the nature of the cure (Forrester, J. 1980 Pp. 2). Freud's paper on neurosis in 1893 suggested that the theory of neurotic symptom includes language as an essential component as each symptom is constructed on the basis of certain ideas. The concept of free association was born as a way of investigating the patients' mental structures. The technique was developed between 1892 and 1898 (Laplanche, J. & Pontalis, J.-B. 2006 Pp. 169) as a means for the patient to say whatever he or she felt without censorship. It is demonstrated within the Studies on Hysteria (1895) that Freud developed this technique by investigating the unconscious as it required the patient to concentrate on a given idea. Freud discovered that this method of investigation achieved a level of insight into the patient's unconscious. According to Freud the unconscious system is a timeless agent of the mind (Freud 1915 Pp. 187). For example, an act of sexual disgust that had taken place years before the patient's analysis may still influence the patient to the present day of treatment; this would have been typically what Freud would have called repressed memories (Freud 1915 Pp. 166). With free association employed, Freud was able to dissect the patient's thought processes as it also gave an insight to the patient's earlier years. This is what was hoped to have been achieved with Anna O.

However, although free association is a method of investigating unconscious activity of memories within thought, 'repression is essentially a process affecting ideas on the border between the system unconscious and preconscious (conscious)' (Freud 1915 Pp. 180). According to Freud there is a level of communication between the two systems. The unconscious influences the preconscious and it is also subjected to influences from the preconscious, each to certain degrees (Freud 1915 Pp. 190). This further suggests that mental activity moves in two opposite directions: *'it starts from the instincts and passes through the system unconscious to conscious thought-activity; or, starting from the outside it passes through the conscious and preconscious until it reaches the unconscious cathexes of the ego and object'* (Freud 1915 Pp. 204).

Relationship between the conscious and unconscious systems

Freud theorises that the anatomical position of the conscious mental activity is regulated via the cortex whilst the unconscious processes via the subcortical parts of the brain (Freud 1915 Pp. 174). This parallels modern neuropsychological explanations of cognitive function. For example, Rita Carta (1998) locates conscious activity emerging from the cerebral cortex and in particular the frontal lobes, as this region is also responsible for conscious perception of emotion and the ability to attend and to focus (Carta, R. 1998 Pp. 298). Carta also distinguishes between different areas of the cortex owing to them the function of specific conscious responsibilities that regulate the system at different capacities. For example, the orbito-frontal cortex inhibits appropriate actions, freeing us from the tyranny of our urges.

The unconscious system is more deeply embedded within the brain; two such areas shall be further elaborated. The cerebellum (mechanical and unconscious system that governs basic behaviour) and the amygdala (reminiscence of a fearful experience that reconstitutes the body state – pumping heart, sweaty palms and so on – that arose with the original experience).

LeDoux (1996) pieces together a theory of how the conscious system interlinks with the unconscious system providing a framework that demonstrates the importance of conscious processing within free association, and in turn, how free association relies on conscious activity for an accurate reconstruction of repressed memories. According to LeDoux the thalamus receives information; if that information causes anxiety it shunts it to the amygdala and visual cortex. The amygdala registers the information as danger and triggers fast reaction which then the individual considers the response consciously (Carta, R. 1998 Pp. 152). However, the information is logged into the unconscious and over a matter of time repressed and defined as an unconscious impulse manifesting itself on an emotional level.

Unconscious memories are particularly formed during stressful events due to the economics of behavioural functioning. The reason for this is that it is a more efficient way of interacting with the environment as information does not need to be processed in a conscious cognitive way each and every time danger is present as LeDoux has demonstrated (Carta, R. 1998 Pp. 152). Therefore, the unconscious serves as a hard-wired processing system that relies on the hormones and neurotransmitters that when released at times of danger provides information that makes the amygdala more excitable. In this way they also affect the processing of conscious memories (Carta, R. 1998 Pp. 153). As a memory becomes conscious the reconstruction of an event may have an emotional attachment, which stems from the unconscious, however, it is due to it becoming conscious that the individual can perceive the threat and decide how to avoid future threats.

During free association the unconscious thoughts that arise within the session serve as an insight to the patient's life as repressed memories. This process relies on the patient's ability to speak and comprehend text and context. Cognitive functioning of language is invariably a vital tool in the process of liaising information to the therapist.

Wenrnicke's aphasia

Wernicke's aphasia can be defined as a language deficit usually due to brain lesions in the posterior parts of the left-hemisphere (Gazzaniga, M. 2002 Pp. 355). People with Wernicke's aphasia make errors within speech production that are known as semantic paraphasias, speech is often gibberish. Words are jumbled together in an incoherent sequence and frequently new words are invented with no apparent meaning at all (Greenfield, S. 2000 Pp. 13).

The Wernicke's area includes the posterior third of the STG (Gazzaniga, M. 2002 Pp. 387). Language deficits also arise from damage to the junction between the parietal and temporal lobes, including the suramarginal and angular gyri. The Wernicke's area is situated within the left hemisphere of the posterior region of the brain and regulates language comprehension (Gazzaniga, M. 2002 Pp. 387).

According to Ornstein's (1997) research on right-side and left-side hemispheric function, he hypothesizes that the left side is mostly responsible for 'text' and verbalisation, whilst the right-side is responsible for 'context' and emotional processing. However, there is interaction between the two sides, for example, linguistic input processed via the left hemisphere can influence right hemisphere emotional experience (Pally, R. 2000 Pp. 107). The general principle is that although there are specialised arrears that designate a function, the two hemispheric sides work together in unity. In this way, the right-side expresses its dominance of emotion as it is related to bilateral control over the autonomic nervous system and cortisol production and according to Schore (1994) it has a greater connectivity to the limbic structures (Pally, R. 2000 Pp. 108). This can, to a certain degree, explain why there is such an emotional significance of functioning to that part of the brain, it is more involved with the limbic system, which controls emotional behaviour, particularly aggression and sex (Greenfield, S. 2000 Pp. 15).

Visuo-spatial ability correlating with handedness

In order to gain a clear insight to mental processes it is important first to determine a route of investigation that can suggest an empirical finding from overt behavioural analysis.

According to evidence presented by Rita Carta (1998) right-handedness is strongly associated with left-brain dominance (Carta, R. 1998 Pp. 78). Ninety-five percent of right-handers have language firmly lodged only in their left hemispheres. However, left handed people, seventy percent of them have language in the left hemisphere. Of the other thirty percent most of them seem to have language in both hemispheres. The general rule is that language is significantly in the left hemisphere for most of the tested population.

It is suggested that handedness is well established by the time a baby is born. The first signs of it can be seen at just fifteen weeks' gestation when most babies start to show a distinct preference for sucking their thumbs.

The current consensus about left-handedness is that some of it is simply genetically determined and of no particular significance, while in others it is because of some prenatal disturbance that arrests the normal development of the left-brain/right-brain dominance. Marian Annett (1985) imbues an interesting theory of the genotype playing an important role in hand dominance as well as hemisphere dominance. According to Marian Annett's research on visuo-spatial ability in subgroups of left-handers and right-handers, test scores of spatial ability were considered in relation to differences between the hands in skill, a decline of ability with increasing dextrality was found in right-handers and left-handers. In terms of the right shift theory the evidence suggests that there are costs for visuo-spatial ability associated with the presence of the rs+ gene, even in single dose (rs + - genotypes), and that those who lack the gene (rs - - genotype) have advantages for spatial ability. It is hypothesized that when this allele is present on one or both chromosomes some advantage is likely to be conferred on the left cerebral hemisphere which tends to induce speech on that side and incidentally increases the skill of the right hand in comparison with the left hand. *'When the right shift allele (rs+) is absent on both chromosomes, the alternate allele(s) at that locus (rs-) are indifferent or neutral for speech and handedness'* (Annett, M., 1985 Pp. 493).

Results from such investigations of spatial ability and handed preference have given an interesting insight and have supported Marian Annett's theory. From a college study conducted in 2002 students were asked to undergo a series of tests that were designed to gain an accurate reading of their visou-spatial ability in relation to their hand preference and hand ability (Evangelou, P. 2002 Pp. 7). The results were in favour of Annett's theory, with a significant result of $r = .032$ (two-tailed test). This supports Annett's hypothesis that suggest that there is a psychobiological interpretation of hand preference that correlates with one's spatial ability and contributes to a developing theory that lends favour to right hemisphere function in liaising information via picture form.

Marian Annett defines the right shift theory as dependent on the genotype, whether + or -. Consideration of the influence of the environment and social pressures is not widely discussed in her theory.

The left hemisphere in right-handed people is more dominant; it is this hemisphere which is responsible for speech functions, whereas the right hemisphere, unconnected with the activity of the right hands or with speech has remained subdominant. This principle of lateralization of functions has naturally become a new and decisive principle of the functional organisation of the cerebral cortex.

Recent research has shown that the left (dominant) hemisphere in right handed people plays an important role in the cerebral organisation of all higher forms of cognitive activity connected with speech, active verbal memory and logical thought. The right (non-dominant) hemisphere either begins to play a subordinate role in the cerebral organisation of these processes. This lends support in aid of a 'picture drawing method' of therapy for those patients that suffer with Wernicke's aphasia, damage to the left side of the brain that disrupts cognitive functions such as language and consequently destroy a portion of the patient's ability to communicate. However, with new methods employed to communicate via a picture drawing method this should prove to be a more accurate way of liaising information as it requires the attention of the right side of the brain that correlates with handedness.

A case of Wernicke's aphasia: Mrs K's case

An interesting case that clarifies the symptoms of Wernicke's aphasia is exhibited within a Psychoanalytic observation known as case K. This case is of a patient that was recovering from Wernicke's (sensory) Aphasia (Kaplan-Solms & Solms 2005 Pp. 90).

Mrs K was a patient who suffered with Wernicke's aphasia after she had experienced an assault that left her unconscious. According to her case history she fell victim to multiple blows to the head, leaving her unconscious and in a state of trauma (Solms & Kaplan-Solms 2002 Pp. 98). Consequently this affected the way her language was processed and could not speak the same way again. *'A CT scan demonstrated an acute left fronto-parietal subdural haematoma (with slight middle shift) and a left temporo-parietal intracerebral haemorrhage. Intra-operative observation revealed a substantial haemorragic lesion in the mid-temporal area, extending posteriorly to include the supramarginal gyrus. After the operation, a follow-up scan demonstrated an extensive area of low density in the left temporal lobe'* (Solms & Kaplan-Solms 2002 Pp. 92).

As a result of Mrs K's condition she reported two main differences in her daily functioning. The first was the inability to dream and the second was an inability to retain audioverbal material in working memory (i.e. consciousness) (Solms & Kaplan-Solms 2002 Pp. 93). The relationship between words and things had lost its meaning and as a result Mrs K could not verbalise and speak in a fluent way. A typical sentence reported by her therapist had been noted as follows, *"I had a job selling pictures...I mean tickets...books of tickets, till recently..."* (Solms & Kaplan-Solms 2002 Pp. 98). This clearly demonstrates a struggle between text and context of meaning. What is most interesting here is that although Mrs K stated *'pictures'* instead of tickets, she notices that a mistake was made with the wrong word and quickly corrects herself. This demonstrates that although she suffered with Wernicke's aphasia subsequently her consciousness had also been affected. Solms (2002) qualifies this by asserting that Mrs K's conscious system was defective. It was not that she did not have thoughts but rather that she was unable to attach words to her thoughts and therefore was unable to render her thoughts conscious (Solms & Kaplan-Solms 2002 Pp. 109).

This is a typical problem reported by someone that suffers with Wernicke's aphasia. It is suggested that although the processing of words and assigning meaning to those words yields as problematic there is a solution for gaining relevant information from the patient that does not require the employing of words and that is through the proposed theory of picture signalling. Working in much the same way as free association does the patient has the opportunity to express the way she feels by free associating through drawing with emphasis placed on shapes and meaning that derives from objects drawn. This too employs the ability to gain access to repressed material and allows someone with Wernicke's aphasia the flexibility to postulate on suspended thought if need be.

Mrs K's case concluded by demonstrating that there is evidence to suggest that the function of the ego has the quality of being preconscious. Therefore, language processing is not an essential feature for obtaining information from the patient (Solms & Kaplan-Solms 2002 Pp. 114).

A conclusive remark as consideration for further investigation

After considering the evidence provided of a mind-body connection this lends support to a theory that considers another possible way of free associating that does not require the full attention of the Wernicke's area. This to some degree sheds light on an alternative method of free associating by employing a paper and pen method of 'picture drawing'. By utilising the right hemisphere region of the brain that processes visuo-spatial ability and verifying the correlational significance of handedness this should demonstrate a direct link to the individual's unconscious activity as it is suggested that handedness is biologically constructed and sustained via environmental cues. However, although there is evidence that interlinks handedness with spatial ability the theory of a picture drawing method of analysis in place of free association for patients that suffer with Wernicke's aphasia still requires an in-depth investigation and further still a developing theory of analysis of the material provided by the patient. A proposed hypothesis for further practical investigations should be considered in order to provide evidence to strengthen this picture drawing method as a theory of therapy.

There have been developments within psychoanalysis which have employed a picture drawing method as a therapeutic diagnostic tool. For example, Winnicott introduced the squiggle game which was to find appropriate ways of communicating with young children (Abram, J. 1996 Pp. 303). However, this essay seeks to offer support that this method is not just a form of therapy but also offers an insight to a new method of analysis for free association. For this to be achieved it is critical that existing theories of free association are reviewed and developed according to a scientific paradigm that includes and considers nuero-scientific evidence to develop a new method of liaising information from the patient's unconscious to the psychoanalyst.

Freud attempted to demonstrate a science of behaviour in his works 'Project for a Scientific Psychology' (1886-1899). Although Freud abandoned this project it nevertheless asserts a complex mechanical relationship between the mind and brain. With new advances in neuro-psychology it is now possible to investigate the links that gel the human body and mind together by asserting a theory of function that sees a new line of thought for the method of free association. It is only through the employment of scientific measures that this hypothesis can crystallize.

Bibliography

Annett, M. (1970) A Classification of Hand Preference by Association Analysis, British Journal of psychology.

Annett, M. (1985) Left, Right, Hand and Brain: The Right Shift Theory London: Lawrence Erlbaum.

Carta, R. (1998) Mapping the Mind, Weidenfeld & Nicolson Publishers, Great Britain.

Abram, J. (1996), The Language of Winnicott: a dictionary of Winnicott's use of words, Karnac Books, London.

Evangelou, P. (2002) 'Correlation of Spatial Ability, Hand Preference and Hand Skill', Undergraduate Study, Rights Reserved Birkbeck College, Great Britain.

Forrester, J. (1980) Language and the Origins of Psychoanalysis, The Macmillan Press Ltd, London.

Freud, S. (1895) Re-published 2001 'Project for a Scientific Psychology', The Standard Edition of the Complete Psychological Works. Strachey, J., ed., in collaboration with Freud, A., Volume one, Vintage Publications.

Freud, S. (1915) Re-published 2001 'The Unconscious' The Standard Edition of the Complete Psychological Works, Strachey, J. ed., in collaboration with Anna Freud., Volume fourteen, Vintage Publications, Great Britain.

Gazzaniga, M., Ivry. R., and Mangun, G. (2002) Cognitive Neuroscience, The Biology of the Mind, W. W. Norton and Company, New York/London.

Gray, J. A. & Buffey, A. W. H. (1990) Sociology, Haralambos, Unwin Hyman Ltd,

Greenfield, M. 2000, the Human Brian a guided tour, A Phoenix Paperback, Great Britain.

Kaplan-Solms, K. & Solms, M. (2005) 'Clinical Studies in Neuro-Psychoanalysis, Introduction to a Depth Neuropsychology'. Second Edition, Karnac Books, Great Britain.

Laplanche, J., and Pontalis, J.-B. (2006) The Language of Psychoanalysis, Karnac books, London.

Pally, R. (2000) The Mind-Brain Relationship, Karnac Books, Great Britain.

Winnicott, D. W. (1971) Reprinted 2005, Playing and Reality, Routledge Classics, , London and New York.

www.ingramcontent.com/pod-product-compliance
Ingram Content Group UK Ltd.
Pitfield, Milton Keynes, MK11 3LW, UK
UKHW041435180426
11947UKWH00007B/454